The Tourname

Julian Atterton is a young writer
his wife in a remote house on the North Yorkshire Moors and spends his time writing and researching into medieval history. He has studied at the Sorbonne in Paris and at the Universities of Cambridge and East Anglia. His interests include rock climbing, archaeology and acting.

JULIAN ATTERTON

The Tournament of Fortune

Richard Drew Publishing
Glasgow

First published 1985
by Julia Macrae Books

This edition first published 1988 by

Richard Drew Publishing Limited
6 Clairmont Gardens, Glasgow G3 7LW
Scotland

The publisher acknowledges the financial assistance of the Scottish Arts Council in the publication of this book.

British Library Cataloguing in Publication Data

Atterton, Julian
The tournament of fortune.
I. Title II. Series
823'.914[F]

ISBN 0-86267-220-1

Printed and bound in Great Britain by
Cox & Wyman Ltd., Reading

THE ENGLISH AND SCOTTISH BORDERS 1314

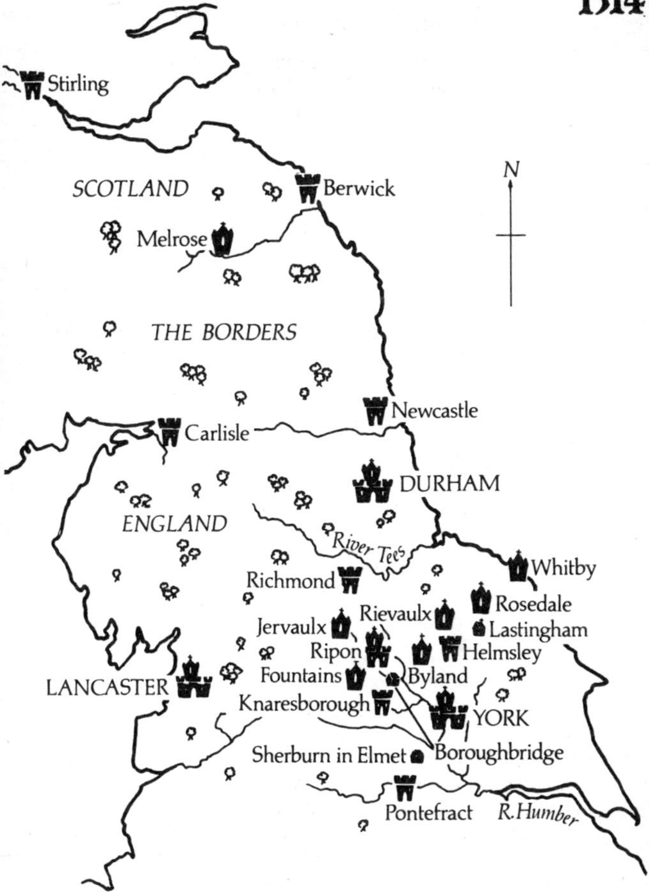

I MUST HAVE BEEN about five years old when Edward Longshanks died and Edward of Caernarvon was crowned King of England.

All I remember is the way people talked of it in the stables and kitchens of the Castle of Richmond: sadly, but as if it were the best thing that had happened since the birth of Christ. The young King, they told me, would quickly end the war with Scotland that was six years older than I was, and when that happened, Count John would ride back to Richmond where he belonged, and my father would ride with him.

All I knew about my father was that his name was Sir Stephen de Falaise and that he served in the garrison of Stirling, one of the great northern castles where the banner of the Three Lions of England was kept flying over the land of the Scots. All I knew about Scotland was that it was somewhere far to the north, where the birds went every spring and where the natives were hairier than dogs and crueller than Saracens.

Years went by, the war dragged on, and slowly I learnt more about it. By the time I was eight, people were saying that young King Edward would never conquer Scotland as long as he preferred fighting his own barons. When I was nine, I learnt that between Richmond and the border was Northumberland, and that the Scots had come south and burnt it. When I was ten, I learnt that between Richmond and Northumberland was a city called Durham, and that the Scots had burnt that too. Carrying mortar buckets for the masons who were hired to repair our walls, I learnt that between Richmond and Durham there was only the river Tees and a day's ride. The talk was all of Robert Bruce, the King of Scotland, and where he would strike next.

By the time I was eleven the English castles beyond the border were falling one by one, and there was only my father's garrison at Stirling that still flew the banner of Three Lions.

I was twelve when King Edward at last marched north to save it . . .

Chapter One

FALLING BANNERS

AS SOON AS Count John's banner was sighted on the road, word of it went round the castle like a wind. The ladies hurried to their windows, the old men crowded every doorway, and the rest of us ran out into the midsummer rain to splash through the mud of the great court and be at the gatehouse when the knights rode in.

They were a long procession of soaked men who did not even make the effort to hold up their heads. For every mounted knight there was a horse with a man-shaped bundle strapped across the saddle, and others with saddles that were empty. Count John looked to be muttering a prayer of thanks as the walls of Richmond closed around him. I searched the faces of the riders and saw a tall man swathed in a russet-coloured cloak whose bald head was bare to the rain and who met my gaze with an inquisitive frown.

A hand touched me lightly on the shoulder and Father Maurice whispered in my ear. "It is your father," he said. "Go to him."

I reached the tall man as he swung himself slowly out of the saddle and leaned against his horse. "Robert?" he asked, smiling as I nodded. "Yes, you have your mother's eyes."

I offered him my shoulder to lean on but, as he took a step towards me, he coughed and staggered. Another knight sprang past me and grabbed him under the arm to steady him, but not before my father had lurched against his horse and his cloak slipped back to reveal a chest that was a mess of torn chain-mail over bandages dark with dried blood.

"Bless you, Andrew," he said to the knight. "Thank God that's over."

Father Maurice bustled up and took my father by his other arm. "Welcome back, Stephen," he said.

Sir Stephen de Falaise grimaced as the knight and the priest straightened his arms across their shoulders. "Maurice," he asked softly, "the old room?"

"I have kept it ready," said the priest.

I took hold of the bridle of my father's horse and watched as they carried him across the great court towards the stairway to the upper room in the tower of St. Nicholas where I was born the day my mother died.

The rain had stopped by evening, and as I came out from supper the long summer twilight was turning the stones of the castle the colour of rust. The knight I now knew to be Sir Andrew Harclay of Cumberland was sitting on the lower steps of the stairway of the tower, intent on the dregs of a goblet of wine.

"Is my father awake yet?" I asked.

Harclay nodded. "Father Maurice is with him now."

"Then I will help with the bandages." I started up the stairway but Harclay grabbed me by the ankle and stopped me.

"The priest is not dressing his wounds. He is giving him the last rites."

I backed down the steps to the ground.

"Sit down," said Harclay. "He will want you as soon as it is over."

Squatting on the step, I studied the knight. His broad shoulders were slumped and his hands lay heavily on the goblet wedged between his knees, but his eyes darted restlessly around the great court as though he were haunted by thoughts that gave him no peace.

"Were you with my father in the garrison at Stirling?" I asked.

He shook his head. "We met on the flight south, and if we had not joined forces when we did, we would neither of us have reached England. We were less than two leagues from the border when we fell into the ambush where your father got his wounds."

"Why was . . .?" I began, only to bite my lip before I said something tactless.

"Spit it out," said Harclay grimly.

"Why was the battle lost?"

It took him a long while to answer. "Robert Bruce's cunning," he said eventually, "and the cunning of Earl Thomas of Lancaster."

I was surprised; not by what he said about Robert Bruce, whose cunning was legendary, but by his slander against Earl Thomas, who I had only ever heard spoken of as a hero, as the one baron who stood against King Edward and stopped him ruling England with utter tyranny.

"But Earl Thomas did not ride with the King," I protested.

"There you have it," snapped Harclay. "He sat in his castle and watched us go, and made certain that all the knights who owe him loyalty stayed behind with him. If he had come with us we would have been an army of all England. We would have been unstoppable." He turned to glare at me with red-rimmed, grey eyes. "But that would not have given Thomas what he wanted – the sight of Edward running home from a disaster."

Just then Father Maurice came down from the stairway. "Sir Stephen is asking for you," he told me. As I climbed past him, he avoided my eyes and my mind raced ahead to the room I was about to enter. My father would be giving me his sword for the day when I followed him to knighthood, and I wondered what I was expected to say.

There was only one small arched window in the upper room, facing east where the sky was already dark, and a rush-light was burning which flickered as I closed the door behind me. My father was propped up with pillows and sat staring at the tapestry of a forest in springtime which covered one of the walls.

"Your mother made it," he said as I followed his eyes to the blue and yellow flowers which clustered around the roots of the trees. "She said it was to make our chamber into a bower." He pointed to the foot of the bed. "Sit there where your face is in the light."

For a while we sat in silence looking at each other. My father was struggling to breathe, and his hands were clenched on the coverlet.

"When I left for Scotland you were still clumsy on your feet," he said.

"I can ride now, Father, and fish."

"Is that so?" He coughed painfully. "At least I have lived long enough to see you again."

"You will not be unavenged, Father," I promised. "When I am a knight, I will make it my quest to win back Stirling for England and for the honour of our name."

He watched me blankly through the gloom, then pointed behind me. "Bring me my sword."

I crossed to the wooden chest over which the priest had laid my father's clothes and picked up the long sword in its scabbard of red leather. My father clasped it to his chest so that he looked like one of the stone figures on the tombs of the crusaders.

"Place your hand beside mine and listen to me. I have played little part in your life, Robert, but I want to bind you to me with an oath. You must swear, on this sword, to obey my will. It is the only thing I will ever ask of you, and if you obey me, I will die in peace."

I swelled with pride and found exactly the right words for my answer. "Father, my oath is yours for the asking."

"Good," he said, and gazed at me so intensely that his eyes seemed to bite into my head. "This is my will, that when I am dead you will travel to the Abbey of Fountains and vow yourself to the Order of St. Bernard."

"A monk?" I yelped. "You want me to become a monk? You cannot mean it!"

"Your oath, Robert. Give it to me."

"No!" I wailed. "Never!"

My father seized my wrist in a grip that pinched me to the bone, and pulled me towards him.

"Listen, boy, you are the only treasure I have left and I know what I am asking. You are twelve years old and too young to find your way in the world." I tried to wriggle out of his grip but he held me down. "You will go to the Abbey of Fountains until you are old enough to know the True Wheel. Then and then only will you be ready to choose your quest in life. Now, give me your oath."

His grip tightened. "I swear it," I sobbed. "I swear it, Father."

He gasped and fell back against the pillows, racked with coughing and breaking out in sweat. When the coughing stopped, the coverlet was specked with blood.

"Ask Andrew Harclay to come to me," he said, and as I paused in the doorway to look back he raised his hand in farewell. "Find the True Wheel, Robert, and may God be with you."

Harclay was still at the foot of the stairway. I mumbled out my message and began to run fast across the great court and up onto the deserted wall where I leaned over the battlements so that no one could see my face.

Away over the Pennine Hills the sun was sinking in a

wine-coloured glow. The river that snaked around the foot of the castle outcrop was vanishing into the shadows. From across the valley came the chime of the bells of St. Martin's Priory, and turning towards the sound I saw the white canons crossing the great court to sing Compline in the chapel. They made my flesh creep. All my childhood I had dreamed of knighthood, of noble adventures and deeds of arms. To be the prisoner of white robes and a vow of silence seemed like living death: my father might as well have sewn me in a sack and thrown me into the river. I turned back towards the sun and wished I could sink with it.

It was almost dark when I heard tired footsteps behind me and Harclay came onto the rampart. "Stephen is dead," he said, and signalled to me to follow him down.

By the time we had reached the foot of the steps, my mind was made up.

"Sir," I said, "you are a knight and I am a knight's son. Will you make me your squire and take me with you until the day comes when I am ready for knighthood?"

He stopped and gave me a long, cold look. "A fair try, though it does you no honour. If I said yes we would both be breaking an oath. Before he died I gave your father my word that I would deliver you myself to the Abbey of Fountains."

By noon the next day the funeral Mass had been sung and my father laid to rest in the hallowed ground by the chapel. As the grave was filled in, I turned to see a groom waiting with a fine palfrey for Harclay and a thick-legged hackney for me. Count John watched as we mounted, and when we were ready he handed Harclay a small leather purse.

"In there are ten marks of silver for the Abbot," he told me. "I cannot have the son of a knight asking monks to take him in without a gift of patrimony. Stephen made a wise choice; prayers are what England needs now, not knights."

They were the nearest thing to kind words that anyone at

Richmond had ever said to me, but even so it was hard to leave. We rode out by the west gate and as we crossed the packhorse bridge over the Swale, I looked longingly back at the castle on its clifftop above the river. It was all I knew.

Our way led up the valley to the priory at Marrick where we took a track south over the hills, and late in the afternoon came down into the wide mouth of Euredale. Pastures filled with sheep gathered for shearing gave way to hayfields and woods, and rising over them all was the castle of Middleham with its keep like a huge square rock.

"Is that where we will spend the night?" I asked eagerly.

Harclay smiled. "Well, well, there was I thinking you were practising your vow of silence. No, we spend the night at the Abbey of Jervaulx. We'll be better fed and lodged there, and as they are white monks you'll get an eyeful of all your tomorrows."

I began to feel glumly curious. "What other vows will I have to make?"

"Poverty and chastity. The first is something of a joke. The white monks own half the North, and Fountains alone has a hundred manors and granges scattered from the Vale of York to the far side of the Pennines."

I saw what he meant when we came in sight of Jervaulx. The abbey church and buildings were as vast as any castle, with window after window and all of them paned with glass. The Vesper bell began ringing as we approached, bringing white monks and brown-robed lay brothers scurrying home across the fields like ants to a nest. I wondered if ten marks of silver would be enough to buy me a place in the Order.

The guest-house lay outside the abbey buildings, and was splendid in itself, with a wide hall, a chimneyed fireplace, and an upper floor for sleeping. We were welcomed by a monk with rickety legs who brought us wine, bread, vegetable stew and a crumbly white cheese before tottering off to take his own meal with his brothers.

There was one other guest, a foreign merchant named Messer Alessandro who described himself proudly as Florentine and who seemed grateful for our company. He had just come from York, and he talked and talked about the parliament there.

"So now your King gives Earl Thomas all he wants," he said, waving a hunk of bread at us. "He says he will banish the favourite, Hugh Despenser, from his court and do nothing without the advice of Earl Thomas. Now tell me, does this mean all is well and that your kingdom will be strong again?"

Harclay laughed bitterly. "If only it did. I know Edward hasn't the strength of his father's shadow, but even he won't live with this for long. He has never forgiven Thomas for killing Piers Gaveston. This will be one more grudge he will store up, and God help the kingdom when the day comes that he is strong enough to settle his scores."

Messer Alessandro made a gesture of lament. "So you are telling me this quarrel will go on forever. What about the Scots? This long war may be giving you many knightly adventures, but the Scottish raids are a plague on the wool trade. It is regrettable that your old king, Edward Longshanks, was so good at war and that his son is so bad at it."

"It's a misfortune when fathers start things that their sons can't finish," agreed Harclay.

"Then again," mused Messer Alessandro, "perhaps it is better to have a king who is too weak than one who is too strong. Have you heard the news from France? King Philippe has burnt the Grand Master of the Templars."

Harclay stiffened. "Burnt du Molay?"

"At the stake, in accordance with the charges of heresy. You have to admire the cleverness of it. If a man is your enemy, convict him of heresy so his land is forfeit to the Crown. It works very well if you happen to be the Crown.

Perhaps your King Edward should try it on the Earl of Lancaster?"

Harclay reached for the wine. "In a world where the Order of Knights Templar can be destroyed none of us are safe."

Leaving them to talk about the evils of the world I stumbled upstairs to sleep. Twice in the night I was woken by the singing of the monks.

We left at daybreak, and soon passed out of Euredale into the rolling fringelands of the Vale of York, where we rode through villages I had never heard of and wide fields of green corn that rippled in the wind. By late morning the wind had died away and the day was turning hot, and as we nudged our horses through a deep ford, the sunlight dancing on the river made my head reel. Harclay reached out to steady me.

"On the far bank we'll stop and eat."

Tethering the horses to the edge of a meadow, we returned to the riverbank and stretched out beside some tattered poppies to make a meal of the bread and cheese we had brought from Jervaulx. By the time we had finished we were both yawning. Harclay lay back with his arm across his eyes and soon began to snore. My eyes went to the purseful of silver that was tied to his belt, and from that to his knife which was lying on the grass beside the remnants of the loaf. I wondered what my chances were of cutting the purse and riding off without waking him, and I was still wondering when I heard horsemen on the far side of the river.

In the distance I saw four riders approaching the ford fast, and a moment later I realised that one of them was galloping for his life and that the other three were hunting him down.

The first rider plunged his horse into the ford and I saw the look of despair on his face as the depth of the water all but brought him to a halt. His pursuers reined in on the bank where one of them leapt from his horse, pulled a longbow from his shoulder and began to load an arrow. I opened my mouth to shout a warning but in the same instant Harclay's hand came down on the back of my neck and shoved me to the ground. Peering through the grass, I saw the rider jerk in the saddle as the arrow caught him in the back. Somehow he swung himself upright and rode on. The second arrow struck him in the neck, and this time he lurched from the horse into the water. The men on the far bank burst out laughing, and the best dressed of them, who wore a yellow surcoat emblazoned with a strange coat-of-arms like six gourds hanging from three sticks, walked over to the archer and clapped him on the back. They were still laughing as they rode away.

"Were they Scots?" I asked.

"No," muttered Harclay. "The one in the yellow surcoat was Girald de Ros, one of Earl Thomas's cronies. Let's go and see who they were hunting."

We ran downstream until we caught up with the body, and Harclay waded out and dragged it to the bank. The rider wore a long jerkin of rough leather, but from his belt hung a knight's sword. Harclay frowned and opened up the leather jerkin, revealing a white surcoat emblazoned with a red cross.

"A Templar," he said. "I should have guessed." He heaved the body back into the river and we watched it drift away.

"What was their heresy?" I asked.

"Don't be a fool," snarled Harclay. He turned on me angrily then checked himself and shrugged. "Why talk about it?"

We rode on, and this time it was Harclay who fell into a silence I could not break. Towards the end of the afternoon we were riding across heathland when a small valley opened up beneath us. We rode down it past neat fields and pastures, and I noticed that the banks of the stream had been walled to control the flow of the water. Then the valley turned and we caught sight of the Abbey of Fountains. It took my breath away. Larger even than Jervaulx, it was a vast building of brown stone which filled the valley from side to side, so completely that even the streams vanished beneath it into arches of stone.

Harclay signalled to me to dismount, and when I had, he tied the reins of my hackney to his saddle. He handed me the purseful of silver, and there he left me.

Chapter Two

THE RULE

ABBOT WILLIAM was the oldest man I had ever seen. The shaved head above his monk's tonsure was as smooth as an egg, but the face below it was as wrinkled as an apple that has sat on a shelf all winter.

"So tell me," he said, "what calls you to the Order of St. Bernard?"

"My father told me to come to you."

"You cannot come here to please your father," said the Abbot gently. "You must come to please God."

"I have brought ten marks of silver," I said, handing him the purse. "Surely that will please God?"

The Abbot's face grew sombre. "And is that all you have to give the brotherhood of monks? I can name you all too many abbeys where silver would make you welcome, but this is not one of them."

I blushed and stared at my feet, wishing I had the courage to tell him he was a sanctimonious old goat.

"I can tell from someone's face if they have a calling to the cloister," he went on, "and I can see no calling in yours."

Perhaps I should have taken my chance to leave, but instead his words made me prickle with pride.

"What do I need?" I asked him.

"You must be willing to submit to an unwavering discipline, which is the only way to lose yourself and find God.

The Rule we follow is a hard one. There are no comforts and many austerities."

"I am the son of a knight," I protested. "I can find the strength to endure anything."

"Even," asked the Abbot with a sly smile, "the strength to forget you are the son of a knight?"

Over the next few days the Abbot's question acquired all too grim a meaning. Life in the abbey was so strange, such an enclosed and unending cycle of duties and devotions, that it soon became hard to remember that there were other ways to live.

My clothes were taken away and I was given a rough white woollen cassock which made my skin itch. I was told to speak only when spoken to, and nobody spoke to me. At sunset, I was taken up to the long monks' dormitory and given a lumpy mattress on which I was left to lie and listen to the snoring and wheezing of the old men around me.

The days were measured by the bells. They rang at daybreak to call us down into the church to sing Prime, and gave us just enough time to wash in the cloister and swallow some bread and cheese before they called us back to church to sing Mass. Then the brothers gathered in the chapter house, to sit on benches round the walls like rooks on a branch while the Abbot led prayers and held a kind of baronial court where matters of abbey business were raised and resolved.

On my first morning I was named to the brothers, and when the chapter dispersed I was given to Brother Hilarion, the master of novices, whose task was to teach me Latin. Armed with some smelly yellow parchments, he led me to a bench in the cloister and spent a patient hour hammering at my mind with strange words, teaching me the meaning of the prayers and psalms of the Divine Office I would be singing for the rest of my life.

The bells called us back to church, to Terce and High Mass, and only after that did the monks at last file into the refectory for dinner. A monk climbed to a pulpit in the wall to read saintly meditations as we ate, and I had to keep silent my own meditations when a bowl of boiled vegetables was set in front of me and Brother Hilarion whispered that meat was forbidden by the Rule.

No sooner was the meal over than Brother Clarence, the precentor, led me back to the church for a singing lesson. He began by singing a phrase which I then had to copy, and we ended by singing together, listening to our voices as they echoed above us in the heights of the transept.

After the service of Nones, I was sent into the fields with a taciturn lay brother who made me work like a peasant until my back ached and my mouth burned with thirst. I was utterly humiliated, and as if that were not enough for St. Bernard, after Vespers and a supper of yet more vegetables I was made to wash the pots like a common scullion. By the time the bells rang for Compline I was hot, wet, and exhausted, and understood why the older monks were so rickety on their legs as they climbed the stairs back to the dormitory.

I could not sleep. It was the hour when in Richmond Castle the torches were being lit, the wine passed round the great hall, and when Yvain the troubadour would be singing a Breton lay. The air would be rich with the smell of roast game. I groaned and rolled over to bury my head under my pillow. All around me the monks began to snore contentedly.

"Find the True Wheel," my father had said. "Then and then only will you be ready to choose your quest in life."

The following morning I asked Brother Hilarion. He looked puzzled.

"People talk of the Wheel of Fortune, which raises men up and flings them down," he said. "There is truth in the image; you have only to look at the life and death of Piers Gaveston to believe in it. There is also the Blessed Wheel on which St. Catherine was martyred, but which of them is meant by the 'True Wheel' I cannot say. Still, to return to the more important mysteries of the Roman tongue ..."

Brother Clarence could tell me nothing either, and I realised it was not a question that would be answered by monks. It was a riddle, meaningful and meaningless, which kept me awake at night while the days went by, every one of them the same, and I began to sink into a walking sleep in which there was only singing and silence.

Months went by, and the first autumn colours were appearing on the trees that fringed the valley of the abbey when at last something happened which shook me out of my sleep.

It was St. Matthew's Day, and I remember filing into the chapter house expecting a homily on the saintliness of those who abandon worldly wealth to follow Christ. It came as a surprise to see the normally tranquil Abbot William clutching a rosary and looking as if he had just seen the Devil.

"My brothers," he began, "a messenger has come with news so evil I wanted you to be strengthened by Mass before I shared it with you. The Scots have raided further south than ever before. They have burnt many villages and looted our sister abbey of Jervaulx, where I am told they killed nine of the lay brothers ..."

A murmur of shock ran round the chapter house, and several of the monks crossed themselves.

"There is more," he said balefully. "On their ride home their path crossed two of our granges. They burnt them to the ground and killed all they found there. Among the dead is Brother Cyprian our treasurer. So let us pray, let us pray for our brothers and their journey to our Father in Heaven."

The meekness with which the monks hung their heads was

more than I could bear. I began to shake as all the feelings I had been suppressing for months came to the boil inside me.

"How can you?" I yelled, causing a row of startled faces to swing towards me. "How can you sit there as silent as fish? Prayer, prayer, prayer! Prayer is no answer to this."

"Brother Robert, be silent," ordered the Abbot.

"I will not be silent," I shouted back. "How can you sit there like cripples while people are being murdered? This is the richest abbey in the North. Hire soldiers, send them after the Scots and avenge your brothers, but for God's sake do something!"

"Take him to the cells," said Abbot William.

Brother Hilarion and Brother Clarence seized my arms and pulled me out of the chapter house. They marched me along the cloister, through the parlour and into the Abbot's house where they pushed me into one of the penitential cells on the ground floor, all without saying a word. Two bolts were slammed home, locking me in.

"Spineless sheep!" I screamed after the receding footsteps. "Brain lepers!"

The cell was bare except for a stone bench and a small niche of a window, set too high in the wall for me to be able to see out of it. In a corner by the door sat an empty bucket. I walked round in circles until I wore myself out. The bells were ringing for High Mass. I gave in and slumped down onto the bench, where I sat with my head in my hands as the sound of singing began to drift over the abbey.

After a few hours, the only anger left in me was anger at myself for breaking the Rule I had thought I was strong enough to live by.

It was dark, and well past the hour of Vespers when the door opened and Abbot William came in.

"Has your anger left you, Robert?" he asked.

I hung my head. "Yes, Father."

"Good. Follow me upstairs."

A fire had been kindled in the Abbot's chamber. He signalled to me to pull up a stool while he sank into a high-backed chair and stared into the flames.

"If I followed the Rule to the letter," he said with a smile, "I would not allow myself a fire until All Saints' Day. That is still five weeks away, and an inch or two down the blade of our northern winter. I claim it now as a privilege of old age, and justify it by remembering that St. Benedict ordered our Rule while living under the kinder skies of Italy."

"I thought it was St. Bernard who ordered our Rule?" I said.

"It was St. Bernard who renewed it," said Abbot William. "He lived in an age when the monasteries were all in crowded cities, where it was all too easy for the cloister to be a market and the Rule to be forgotten. Bernard turned to the wilderness, to be closer to God and to live the Rule unhindered by the babble of the world. It is because we follow him that we are called Bernardines, but we owe as much to the man who inspired Bernard, whose name was Robert de Molesme." He smiled at my surprise. "Yes, so Robert is a fine name for a white monk, and it is a great pity you have no calling to the cloister."

"It is not that, Father," I protested. "I have tried to live by the Rule, and I'm shameful for my disobedience."

"For calling us as silent as fish?" asked the Abbot. "You paid us a great compliment."

"It is only that I am what I am, the son of a knight. I cannot understand why you let the Scots burn our granges . . ."

"And do nothing but pray," he said, smiling as he finished my sentence for me. "The answer lies in the Rule. We are contemplative monks, and our only power is the power of prayer. The Abbey of Fountains must be a beacon of prayer in a torn world, and that is why the Rule must not be broken. If our prayers are to be powerful, we must be worthy of God.

Through living the Rule we burn our beings as incense in praise of the Lord, and in return for our sacrifice we ask him to hear our prayers for an end to this war between Christians, for a world that is once more made whole." He levelled his eyes on me. "So, Robert, now you must decide if you can make that sacrifice."

I stared into the fire, thinking about my father and wondering if he had known all this and sent me to the abbey not to bury me alive but to set me a challenge. I met the Abbot's gaze. "I still wish to be a novice."

Abbot William blinked. "You do? My, my, that is heartening. On the chest over there is a flagon of spiced wine. Pour me a cup, and pour one for yourself."

I fetched the wine and we sipped it by the fire.

"This means," he said, "that I will have to set you a penance. You know that our lost Brother Cyprian was our treasurer. You will join Brother Ambrose, our librarian, who I have asked to take over the accounts. There is much sorting out and copying to be done, and believe me, it will be a penance."

Brother Ambrose was one of the oddest monks in the abbey. Short and generously paunched, he waddled along inspecting everyone and everything with eyes like onions which peered out from under eyebrows as thick as brooms. He also had a habit of pouting his lips and looking as if he were kissing the air in front of his face. As we filed out of church after Nones, he stepped out of the line and waited for me in the cloister.

"*Benedicite*," he said.

"*Dominus*," I replied, completing the formal greeting.

"So you're to be my scribe," he said with a disdainful sniff. "I wonder what I have done to deserve this extra burden."

He led me up the day-stairs and along a passage where he unlocked a room with barred windows and shelf upon shelf crammed with rolled sheepskin parchments. A table by a window which looked out onto the roof of the cloister arcade was piled high with scrolls and tally-sticks. Brother Ambrose unfurled a parchment and stared at it with pursed lips.

"This is the muniment room," he announced, "Brother Cyprian's endless penance. In those chests are the deeds to every one of the abbey's properties, and on the shelves are the accounts of what we have tried to make of them over the last one hundred and eighty-two years. It is to be feared that most of this year's accounts perished with our treasurer, so it may be some time before we know how bad things are."

"Bad?" I repeated in bewilderment. "But I thought this was the richest abbey in the North?"

"So it was," said Brother Ambrose, leafing through the scrolls and sorting them into piles. "The days of riches ended twenty years ago, and quite disgracefully, with the wool crop sold off for years in advance to pay for our building debts. It drove Abbot Henry to resign, and his successor lasted less than a year. Finally the Old King had to send in a commissioner. It was most humiliating."

"And now?" I asked.

"Now we have greater troubles," said Brother Ambrose, "far greater troubles. The winters have been growing longer, and the summers wetter, and the heavy rains have been turning our upland granges back to waste. The war has made it hard to find lay brothers, and without them it costs us more to farm our granges than we make from their harvests and wool crops. Brother Cyprian was a worried man."

By the hour of Vespers I had learnt enough to make my head ache. Walking into the church, I looked around me with new insight and saw every stone as a monument to the generations of monks who over a hundred and eighty years had carved the abbey out of the wilderness. I was beginning to understand their quest.

Late that night, when the bells woke us and we filed down

into the choir to sing Matins and Lauds, the singing was like a rainbow coloured by all the emotions the monks never showed in their faces. We sang while the world slept, and the altar candles were the only pools of light in the vast gloom.

Chapter Three

THE LORD OF FORTUNE

FOR THE NEXT four years it was to seem as if only the Devil ruled in England.

All winter it rained, and when spring came it only rained harder. The roads turned to rivers and we lost touch with our granges, and when the Scots came raiding they were hard put to find anything dry enough to burn. The harvest was dire: wheat had to be dried in ovens before it could be ground, and when the bread had been baked there was no goodness in it. By Michaelmas the whole country was facing a winter of famine.

Left to ourselves behind the high walls of the abbey close we were safe enough, but before long the famine came and searched us out. By Christmas there were women and children camped outside the gatehouse in ramshackle wooden bothies. The children had bellies swollen with hunger and wails it hurt to hear, and their mothers told of villages where the people had been driven to eat roots, bark, and carrion. We fed them all, and our own diet reached a level of self-denial that even St. Bernard would have admired. There was nothing more we could do except pray. Masses were sung day and night in the Chapel of Nine Altars.

By winter's end the older monks were going out like candles in the wind. Late in March, on the eve of the Feast of St. Benedict, we lost Abbot William. It was three months before the roads were safe enough for the abbots of Rievaulx and Byland to come and give their blessing to Walter, our prior, and to place the abbot's ring on his finger and the mitre on his head.

Again the harvest failed, and the second famine winter was harsh and pitiless. Whenever we had news of the outside world it was of Scottish raids and disease, of deeds too dark to chronicle. I grew up among old men who spoke longingly of the glorious years of Edward Longshanks and spoke of the future by quoting the Book of Apocalypse.

In all England there was only one knight whose name was spoken with pride – Sir Andrew Harclay, who threw back a Scottish siege and kept the banner of Three Lions flying over the castle of Carlisle. It was not enough. Everywhere else the border no longer existed, and knights cowered in their castles while the North was bled white. When the Pope sent two cardinals to make peace between England and Scotland they never reached the border. They were seized and held to ransom, by an English knight, and as soon as they were freed they ran back to Avignon. It was the shame of the realm.

Amidst all this, a spring came that was dry and warm, and the corn came up strong and wholesome. The beggars left their bothies by the gatehouse to see if anything was left in their homes, and word trickled in from our farthest granges. Seven had been burnt, and in others the famine had taken two thirds of our flocks, but there were enough new lambs to make Brother Ambrose sit back from his parchments in the muniment room and say a prayer of thanks.

But as the land awoke from its sleep, so did the quarrel between King Edward and Earl Thomas. Every traveller to the abbey brought a new rumour – that the Earl's wife had run away with one of the King's knights – that the King was mustering an army in York – that Earl Thomas was mustering an army – that the King had marched his army past the Earl's castle of Pontefract as a show of strength and a challenge to open war . . .

And while the King and Earl Thomas stalked around baring their fangs at each other, the Scots sank their fangs into the North. The day before my sixteenth birthday we heard that Robert Bruce had captured the border fortress of Berwick, and a few weeks later the Scots raided so far south that they passed within a day's ride of the Abbey of Fountains.

One autumn day I was in the cellarer's yard making a tally of the harvest produce that had come in from the granges when through the gatehouse of the abbey rode a cavalcade of armed men.

I froze in my footsteps. At their head rode a knight with a golden beard and carefully groomed hair that flowed over his shoulders, and who looked around him lazily as though the abbey were his to do whatever he wanted with. His riders wore a rich livery of argent and azure.

"Holy Mary," I whispered. "Robert Bruce?"

"Not that demon," said Brother Martin the cellarer, "but another as bad. You are looking at Thomas of Lancaster."

I turned and fled into the abbey in search of Abbot Walter, and found him in the Chapel of St. Bernard where he was poring over his missal.

"Father, Earl Thomas is here."

Abbot Walter looked up placidly. "Calm yourself, Robert. It's hardly the Day of Judgement. I imagine he has brought half his private army and expects us to feed them?"

"Yes Father, but Brother Anselm the guest-master is still sick in the infirmary."

"Then you can be guest-master. Welcome them and see to their needs, but ask no questions. Earl Thomas will tell us in his own good time why he has decided to grace us with a visit."

All afternoon I scurried to and fro between the guest-houses, the kitchen, and the cellarer's stores. The Rule ordered that guests be received as royally as possible, and the sight of the cooks spitting an ox and plucking chickens was enough to make me whimper with jealousy. All my dealings were with the Earl's steward, and when I visited the guests after Compline to check they had all they needed for the night, I was surprised to be told that Earl Thomas wished to speak with me and that I would find him in the upper chamber.

I found him sunk into a chair with his legs stretched out towards the fire. The candles I had set out had not been lit, and in the shadowy corner beyond the chimney a dwarf sat on a stool, piping on a thin flute. Earl Thomas sat up and took a draught from a goblet of wine.

"Ah, Brother Guest-master," he said, with a voice of exaggerated courtesy. "A few hours here and the peace of your abbey has mellowed my mind. Before you came in I was watching the flames and saying what wisdom it would be to leave my worldly cares behind and float through a cloister in long white robes."

"You would never again eat roast ox," I replied.

He pretended to give this serious thought. "Perhaps that would be too high a price to pay for peace of mind? Perhaps I will ride along the Wheel and leave the day after tomorrow as I planned."

I caught my breath. "Does your lordship call the Wheel you are riding the True Wheel?"

"Oh yes," he said, looking at me curiously. "The Wheel of Fortune is as true a path through life as the way of St. Bernard. I can feel it turning at every hour of the day and the night."

"But does it not throw men down?" I asked. "The way it threw down Piers Gaveston?"

The Earl's teeth gleamed through his beard as he grinned. "Most certainly. Our King thinks I killed Gaveston, but it was the Wheel of Fortune that killed him. You have to be strong to ride the Wheel: strong enough to hold on when it spins you down and grinds you under; strong enough to cling to the spokes until it spins you back to power. That is what separates me from worms like Gaveston."

"And what does it give you to make all that worthwhile?" I asked.

He looked at me askance. "Is it really so far beyond the mind of a monk? It gives me power, a mastery over Fortune herself. Those men downstairs who wear my livery; they follow me because I pay them regularly and feed them well, but more than that, they follow me for my Fortune."

The dark of his eyes glinted with firelight as he stared at me. I knew what I wanted to say – that it made him so obsessed with himself that he was blind to the agonies of England – but I also knew my place.

"Your lordship sent for me," I mumbled menially.

"Ah yes. Tell your treasurer to come to me tomorrow morning. There are matters I have to discuss with him. That is all. You may go."

"He must wish to make the abbey a gift," I suggested to Brother Ambrose as we walked towards the guest-houses the following morning.

He grunted non-commitally and steadied the wobble of his paunch. "When you get to my age, Robert, you may find that your belief in God is far stronger than your belief in the generosity of His creatures, especially when they have private armies to pay for."

Earl Thomas was waiting for us in the upper chamber, where he offered us some of the abbey's wine before broaching the subject of his business.

"As you may know," he began, "a few years ago it pleased

God to bring me the lordship of Lincoln to add to my lordships of Lancaster, Leicester, and Derby. Whilst going over the deeds of my new lands, it came to the attention of one of my clerks that the manors of Wiggesham and Norton were long ago leased to your abbey to use as granges. The lease was for ninety-nine years and expired some twenty years ago. It would please me if you would either return the granges to me or continue to work them and send me the produce."

"Your lordship is quite mistaken," said Brother Ambrose. "The manors of Wiggesham and Norton came to this abbey as free gifts to be ours in perpetuity."

"I fear not," said Earl Thomas with a wide smile. He opened a small chest and produced two scrolls of parchment. "Here are the deeds of the manors in question."

As Brother Ambrose studied the scrolls his lips pursed and pouted, and he handed them back to the Earl with a look of withering disdain. "Obviously the deeds of the manors were stored at the Cluniac abbey near your lordship's castle of Pontefract, and when your clerks asked to see them, the monks could not find them. That is the only reason I can suggest for their having provided your clerk with these blatant forgeries. The parchment they are written on is less than five years old."

Earl Thomas faltered for the merest instant. "Certainly the parchment is new. These are copies. Surely you did not expect me to hazard the originals on the road in such dangerous times as these?"

"Then the originals they are copied from are also forgeries," countered Brother Ambrose. "We have the true deeds here in the abbey, and I can assure you they say something quite different."

"Perhaps they are the forgeries?" suggested the Earl in a voice that was thickening with menace. "Perhaps one of your long-dead predecessors allowed his love of land to get the better of his morals? Be so good as to bring them to me for inspection."

Brother Ambrose stood up and pushed me towards the door. "We will provide your lordship with copies so that your clerk can add them to his records."

"You will do better than that," said Earl Thomas icily. "You will give me the originals, and you will do it by sunset."

Brother Ambrose stormed out of the guest-house and I had to run to keep up with him. Within a few minutes we were in the Abbot's chamber and Brother Ambrose was shaking from head to toe as he poured out an account of what had happened.

"This is barefaced robbery," he thundered. "How are we meant to survive with the Scots burning our granges to the north and the magnates of the realm stealing our granges to the south?"

Abbot Walter sighed. "Well, at least it explains why he came. I had a feeling it was not for the good of his soul. Are they important granges?"

"Vital," said Brother Ambrose. "At Norton we mine the coal we sell to the ironstone workers, and Wiggesham is our stone quarry. I have just made arrangements with the Archbishop of York for him to buy the stone he needs for his building work from us. After our wool granges they are the richest lands we have."

"And you are certain the Earl's claims are false?"

"False? They stink like a cesspool in August."

"I see," murmured the Abbot. "Then tonight you must tell him so, and we must pray he leaves it at that."

All afternoon I sat in the muniment room, scratching away with goose quill and penknife, making copies of the deeds by which the granges had been granted to the abbey one hundred and twenty years before. I was guilty of pride as I looked over the finished work – four years with Brother

Ambrose had turned me into a capable scribe – and I was disappointed when Earl Thomas gave the parchments the briefest of glances when we took them to him after Vespers.

"Wishful forgeries," he declared, tossing the deeds to the floor. "You disappoint me."

"They are the truth," said Brother Ambrose, "and they are all you will get."

Earl Thomas leaned back in his chair and half-closed his eyes. "This is regrettable. You leave me with no choice but to petition the next parliament to examine both sets of deeds and decide which are genuine."

Brother Ambrose could find no reply and I knew we were sharing the same thought: that the next parliament would do whatever Thomas of Lancaster wanted it to.

At that moment the door flew open and a knight strode in. My eyes went straight to the coat-of-arms emblazoned on his surcoat: a strange design like six gourds hanging from three sticks which I had first seen across a river on a summer's day. One look at his face and I knew he was the same man who had murdered the Templar, only this time he was scowling instead of laughing.

"Girald," snarled Earl Thomas. "What is the meaning of this?"

"I come from York, sire," said Girald de Ros, "with news that could not wait. They have made Badlesmere Steward of the Household."

Earl Thomas gripped the arms of his chair and cursed. "The moment I turn my back," he muttered. "And what is their answer to my claim that, as Steward of the Realm, it is my right to name the Steward of the Royal Household?"

"They say they will search the records and find the precedent."

"And in the meantime that slug Badlesmere . . ." The Earl's face twisted into an expression of disgust. "Edward and Despenser must be laughing tonight."

"This is also the work of Pembroke and the bishops," said de Ros. "They are getting stronger."

Earl Thomas's eyes ranged around the room until they fixed on us. "Get out," he ordered. "Out of my sight."

Brother Ambrose bowed ceremoniously and moved slowly towards the door. "Look and learn, Robert," he said to me in the loudest of whispers; "there is nothing so fierce as the anger of cheated greed."

I lay awake for hours thinking of Thomas of Lancaster and Girald de Ros. If they were the custodians of the True Wheel then I no longer wished to find it.

Just before dawn I smelt burning. All around me the monks were snoring peacefully, but as I lay there the smell grew stronger. Slipping on my shoes I tiptoed down the night-stairs into the church. There was nothing but coolness, stillness, and the smell of burnt-out incense. I opened the door into the cloister and walked out into a cloud of acrid smoke. It was streaming out from under the door of the library, which lay between the church and the chapter house. Out of the corner of my eye I saw a dwarf-like shape run along the south side of the cloister and disappear into the outer parlour, and in the same instant I began yelling the alarm at the top of my voice.

Within minutes there was a chain of monks and lay brothers passing buckets and basins of water from the stream to the cloister, but it was already too late. The oak door cracked and shuddered as the library became an inferno, and the stench of burning sheepskin stung our throats and our eyes. We drenched the door with water and when we kicked it in, it was like opening an oven. A gust of heat sent us staggering backwards and a thousand red cinders blew out into the cloister. All that was left of the library was a shell of blackened stone.

"My books," wailed Brother Ambrose. "My beautiful books."

I told Abbot Walter about the figure I had seen running away. He bent down and examined the floor tiles.

"Look. There is a smear of pitch where whoever it was must have poked the kindling rag under the door. But why in God's name . . .?"

"Earl Thomas," said Brother Ambrose. "He must have thought our deeds to the granges were stored in the library."

Abbot Walter nodded grimly. "Then at least we can go and burn his satisfaction."

We marched across to the guest-houses but they were empty. Earl Thomas and his men were gone. Behind us in the abbey someone tolled the bells of Prime.

Nothing more was said until after Mass, when we gathered in the chapter house with the reek of fire still hanging in the air. When our prayers were over there was a long moment of silence in which we all watched Abbot Walter as he sat with his head back and his eyes closed; and when at last he opened them, I was the first person he looked at as he gazed at each of the brotherhood in turn.

"The way of St. Bernard has always been the way of the wilderness," he said wistfully; "of the face turned away from the world to see nothing but God. It hurts me to have to ask any of you to return to the world, however briefly and however vital the mission, but that is what I now ask two of you. A parliament will be held next spring in York, where Thomas of Lancaster will turn his power against us. You, Brother Ambrose, must be there to fight him. Earl Thomas has enemies; you must find them and persuade them to help us." His eyes came back to me. "And you, Brother Robert, must go with him for a humbler but equally important purpose. You will work in the library of the Abbey of St. Mary, where you will make copies of some of the texts and chronicles we have lost in the fire."

The Rule ordered silent obedience but I could not hide a look of dread.

"And when you return," he said with a smile, "your five years as a novice will be over, and you will be ready to make your vows and join the Order."

Chapter Four

THE GARLAND

ON THE FIRST DAY of May, Brother Ambrose and I set out into the world.

The further we rode from the abbey, the further we rode from silence. Our first miles were through quiet country, through green spring and birdsong, but by noon we were wiping dust from our eyes on a wide road teeming with traders' carts and cattle drovers on their way to the royal market at York.

At the end of the road lay the city: an enchanted vision of creamy-white battlements and soaring above them the towers and spires of more churches than I could count, all of which vanished as we passed through the towered gateway into crowded narrow streets where everyone was in a hurry and everyone shouted. The last mile of the journey was a sordid jostle which brought us bedraggled and sweaty to a house with the emblem of Fountains carved on the gable-beam and where Brother Ambrose slid from his saddle with a grunt of relief.

The door was opened by a woman in her middle years with lively eyes and a starched white head-dress.

"Ah, Mistress Matilda," said Brother Ambrose. "Thanks be to God we have arrived in one piece."

"A far bigger one than when I last saw you," she replied. "How you get so fat on a diet of cabbages I'll never know." She turned to me. "And what's your name?"

"Brother Robert," I replied. It was the first time in almost five years that I had spoken to a woman.

"Well, come inside. I won't eat you. I've a boy who'll see to the horses."

She led us into a low-raftered hall with a fireplace, a long table and some chairs.

"I've cleaned this house from top to bottom," she told us. "You should have seen the dust that had settled in the three years since Abbot William was here, God rest his soul. How long will you be staying?"

"It could be several months," said Brother Ambrose, sinking into a chair with a sigh of contentment.

"You'll be well looked after," said Mistress Matilda.

It was no idle boast. She served us a supper of spiced vegetables stewed in wine, followed by slices of apple and cinnamon pie the size of axe-blades, and by the time she said goodnight and set off for her own home, I was beginning to wish our mission to York could last for a year.

We said Compline in a small room which served as a chapel, and was bare except for a small altar and a statue of Our Lady Mary, then made our way upstairs to bed.

Long after the curfew had been rung, I lay awake listening to the sounds of the city. Drunks staggered singing along the street, tom-cats yowled from the roof-tops, and just when things were quietening down, a man and a woman in the house next door began a loud and complicated quarrel about money. The city was like a book with a hundred stories, so compelling that I suddenly understood why Robert de Molesme had founded his abbey in the silent marshlands of Citeaux.

At cockcrow we sang Prime in the chapel, and at the hour when our brothers at Fountains would be filing into the chapter house, we set out into the city.

"Now, Robert," said Brother Ambrose protectively, "keep your hood up and your eyes on the ground."

I could hardly obey. The great street that led down to the river was crowded, and keeping my eyes on the ground meant bumping into someone with every second step. Besides, there was too much to see: knights and their retinues riding in for the parliament; open shops with every kind of merchandise; bustling women with head-dresses so weird I wondered if they had enormous ears they were trying to hide. The city was a labyrinth of wonders. On the bridge over the Ouse I saw grey friars for the first time, and stared into their faces as though I could learn from their expression what it was that made them believe the way of St. Francis so much holier than the way of St. Bernard. Entering the cathedral close, I gazed open-mouthed at the Minster of St. Peter and the tiny figures of the masons at work on their wooden platforms a hundred feet above the ground.

The hall of the Archbishop's palace was as crowded as the streets. It took Brother Ambrose several minutes to find an usher, and when he returned his lips were pouting with frustration.

"All these people are waiting for an audience, and Archbishop William is still at High Mass. This is going to take all day."

"Do you think he will help us?" I asked.

"He should. As a man who has been an officer in the King's household there is every likelihood that he loathes Earl Thomas as much as his master does."

"An officer in the King's household?" I repeated in amazement. "How on earth did he become Archbishop?"

Brother Ambrose chuckled. "How else? The King likes his key servants to be rich, and nothing makes a man richer than a bishopric." He winked and whispered in my ear. "At least Archbishop William is a man of some learning. The crony that Edward made Bishop of Durham last year, Louis de Beaumont, is such a gawk that he couldn't even read the Latin of his own consecration speech. When he came to the word 'metropolitanus' he huffed and puffed and finally spluttered 'Let us take that word as read.' "

"But that's wicked," I protested.

"I never said it wasn't," said Brother Ambrose. "Now, let's find a bare patch of wall we can lean against."

The day dragged by as the ushers called out name after name. It was past the hour of Nones when our moment came.

Archbishop William received us in a sumptuously tapestried room, where he sat by a window that gave him a view of the masons at work on the Minster. Behind him in a corner sat a scribe who recorded our names as we knelt to kiss the Archbishop's ring.

"May Our Lady bless your Grace," said Brother Ambrose in his humblest voice.

"And may St. Peter watch over your abbey," replied the prelate. "How can I help the monks of St. Bernard?"

As Brother Ambrose told our story, I studied the Archbishop. He was a tall man with a surprisingly quiet voice and a tuft of silvery beard that made him look more like a baron than a churchman. When the story reached the burning of our library, his face wrinkled with disgust.

"And so, your Grace," finished Brother Ambrose, "we beg for your help in stopping this oppression of Holy Church."

Archbishop William beckoned to his scribe and whispered in his ear, and as the scribe hurried out of the room he turned to us and smiled comfortingly.

"You must not worry about Earl Thomas," he said. "He is not the man he used to be."

"But what if parliament decides that his deeds are the true ones?" asked Brother Ambrose.

The Archbishop shook his head. "Things are not the way they were two years ago," he said. "Thomas is too busy haggling about his rights as Steward of the Realm to have time for anything else." He sat forward, and a look of prophecy came into his eyes. "I can tell you what the outcome of this parliament will be – the marching north of the King with all the earls and knights of the land in one army, to recapture the fortress of Berwick and throw Robert Bruce back into Scotland. Once that is achieved, the realm of England will heal itself and nothing must interfere with that purpose. Do you understand me?"

"Then what would your Grace have us do?"

"Keep silent and wait. I will see that your granges are not stolen in this parliament, and by the autumn Earl Thomas will not have the strength to harass anyone."

The scribe came back into the room and handed the Archbishop a purse which he gave to Brother Ambrose. "Here is a gift towards the renewal of your library. Remember me in your prayers, and forget to replace any lost chronicles of the time of William Fitzherbert."

He held out his ring for us to kiss, and with that we were ushered out of his presence.

"What did he mean?" I asked as we left the palace. "What are the lost chronicles of William Fitzherbert?"

Brother Ambrose chuckled. "A fine old story. When our abbey was less than ten years old, a certain William Fitzherbert was made Archbishop of York. He was such an outrageous scoundrel that our Abbot got St. Bernard himself to make the Pope annul the appointment. The quarrel lasted for years, and even though we lost, God had the last word. Fitzherbert was reinstated, but a month later he dropped dead."

"Then where is the harm in our having chronicles of it if it's all so long ago?"

Brother Ambrose pointed to the Minster. "Because old Fitzherbert is now Saint William of York, with a shrine of marble and jewels. In a good year the pilgrims come in droves, and the money they spend is paying for the building you see going on behind you. Our own Archbishop William knows, and any monk of Fountains should know, that a prayer at the shrine of St. William is not worth a leek, and he has just been reminding us to keep the truth to ourselves."

"But that's wicked," I protested.

"Don't be insolent, Robert. If that is the price the Archbishop asks for his help, then we pay it."

We passed through the gateway of the cathedral close and Brother Ambrose ended the conversation by pulling up the hood of his cowl and hurrying off down the street. I followed in silence, tired and thirsty and with an unwelcome feeling that we were not worthy to follow in St. Bernard's footsteps. I felt as though I had lost something, but I could not find a name for what it was that had gone.

Archbishop William was right in his prediction. The outcome of the parliament was an order to every knight of the realm to muster at Newcastle for the march on Berwick. By the end of May they were gone, leaving York with the royal court and exchequer to keep it bustling, and leaving Brother Ambrose and me copying out manuscripts in the library of St. Mary's Abbey.

As a place to work it was lamentable. The abbey was of the Benedictine Rule, and the monks vowed to silence, but they chattered away their cloister hours and sounded like a flock of hungry ducks. Nor were they fond of white monks. It was from St. Mary's Abbey that thirteen monks had run away to found the Abbey of Fountains. We could see why they had, and the monks of York did not like the look in our eyes that told them so.

The library, though, was a wonder, filled with ancient manuscripts from Rome and Constantinople, with the latest writings from the University of Paris, and with books illuminated in all the colours of the rainbow. Day after day I copied the writings of the Fathers, hoping always that they would speak of the True Wheel, but all that seemed to matter to them was the endless war between God and the Devil that had been raging since the dawn of time.

June went by, and the trees reached the lush green of midsummer, and the books we had bought or copied grew into a small pile which we stored in our chapel. Then one day Brother Ambrose sent me off to work alone, and when I came back in the evening he was lying in bed, groaning and clutching his paunch.

"There is a demon in my stomach," he wailed.

"That is about all it can be," said Mistress Matilda sternly. "There is nothing wrong with my cooking."

"Indeed not," said Brother Ambrose. "No, this is God's punishment for my sin of gluttony."

"Shall I go for a surgeon?" I asked.

"I'm not having some leech prodding at me," he thundered. "All they ever do is tell me I have a choleric humour and that the Sun is in Uranus. Twaddle like that only makes things worse."

So Brother Ambrose kept to his bed and sweated out his fever, while the city sweated out the fever of July and news came from the border that the King's army was laying siege to Berwick. On the tenth day of his illness, Brother Ambrose called me to his bedside.

"There is an errand you must run for me," he said. "Take two marks of silver and go to the house of Jocelin of Bordeaux. He will have some books I ordered from France, and unless we pay him quickly he may sell them to someone else."

The house of Jocelin of Bordeaux stood in one of the narrow alleys between the Thursday market and the cathedral close, where the houses overhung and the gutters stank in the heat. The door was opened by a round-faced servant girl who ushered me into a cavernous hall that was stacked to the roof with barrels of wine.

"Is the master at home?" I asked.

"Oh, the master," she said mournfully, and crossed herself.

"Who is it, Ellie?" called a girl's voice from the far side of an open doorway.

I walked through and found myself in a high-walled rose garden where a girl was sitting on a bench beneath a cherry tree. She was young and pale, with eyes of an unearthly green, and she was dressed in mourning. At the sight of my robes her eyes widened in anger.

"If you're another friar come for money to say Masses you can get out," she snapped. "My father's soul can do without you."

"Is this the house of Jocelin of Bordeaux?" I asked. "I am Brother Robert of the Abbey of Fountains. Master Jocelin has some books for me."

"Books?" she said, and bit her lip. "Books," she repeated, as if trying to gather her wits. "Master Jocelin was buried a week ago. I will see if I can find your books for you."

She hurried into the house, leaving me to slump gratefully into the shade of the tree. Beside me on the bench was an unfinished daisy chain. I picked it up and admired the neatness with which the stems were pinched and the flowers linked into a garland. The girl came back holding a bundle wrapped in cloth.

"These are the only books I could find," she said.

Unwrapping the bundle I found a beautiful gospel and two illuminated psalters. The parchment was unlike any I had ever seen; the pages were each as thin as a leaf and as white as snow.

"This is not sheepskin," I said. "What is it?"

"You're not a very knowledgeable monk, are you?" she asked. "This is paper, made in Castile to a secret that comes from Cathay at the other end of the world. Try not to get it wet. There was a tally with them to say they are worth two marks."

I handed her the money and decided that her eyes were not unearthly but the green of the stems of daisies. I caught her looking at me oddly and fumbled for words. "Your father seems to have been surrounded by beauty."

Her answer was to frown. "Or by hypocrites. I know as well as you do that these books were shipped from France by Eleazar David, but you used my father as go-between to save yourselves from dealing with a Jew."

I was dumbstruck, and at the sight of my confusion she bit her lip again.

"Oh, forgive me," she said. "Ever since my father died I keep wishing I could tear the world to pieces."

"I know," I said, without knowing what I knew. "And it is a hot day," I added quickly.

She cheered up a little. "I like hot days. Where I was born it is as hot as this for most of the year."

"In Bordeaux?"

She nodded. At that moment the street-door opened and closed and a woman dressed in black came into the garden and scowled at the sight of me.

"Marie, what are you doing?" she demanded.

The girl stiffened. "This is Brother Robert from the Abbey of Fountains. He had business with Father."

"Jocelin's business is no affair of yours," sneered the woman. "Give me that money."

The girl called Marie threw it at her. "It is as much my affair as yours," she shouted.

I tucked the books under my arm and rose to my feet. "I must go. It is almost the hour of Vespers." I bowed to the girl. "Please tell Eleazar David that the books are most beautiful." On my way out I made the mistake of trying to smile at the woman. She gave me a glare that was full of venom, and if looks could maim I would have hobbled home on crutches.

Brother Ambrose was propped up in bed sipping barley broth. He unwrapped the books and sighed.

"Excellent. Worth every penny."

"The merchant is dead," I said. "Who was he?"

Brother Ambrose crossed himself. "Poor Jocelin. He was a vintner. The abbey buys its wine from him and he was always willing to find us books and the like."

I wanted to challenge him to tell me about Eleazar David, but as Brother Ambrose leafed through one of the psalters he uttered a mild exclamation and held up a garland of daisies.

"Where did this come from?" he asked.

"Oh that, well quite," I mumbled. "I had to wait in the garden, and I made it while I waited."

He gave a pout of disapproval. "You should spend such moments reciting the psalms. Still, one garland of daisies is hardly enough to throw your soul open to temptation."

It was more than enough. I lay awake that night, searching my memory for the songs the troubadours of Richmond Castle had sung of Bordeaux and the kingdom of Aquitaine; the songs of Eleanor, the queen who had brought England and France to their knees. And when at daybreak I knelt in the chapel and said my first prayer to Our Lady Mary, I spoke the name and my mind flew straight to the girl in the garden. I knew it was blasphemy, but I could not stop myself.

Chapter Five

THE LOVE TOKEN

THE SONGS of the troubadours came back to me one by one – songs of knights ennobled by their love for a woman, doing deeds of courage in the hope of winning love's reward – and they seemed that summer morning to have more meaning than any of the psalms I had learnt from the monks.

Walking through the city I stared at every girl in the streets, believing as I turned each corner that I was about to set eyes on Marie. She was nowhere to be seen, and yet I felt her everywhere; in the shops she must have bought from and the alleys she must have walked through a thousand times. The market-place near her home seemed as sacred as the Chapel of Nine Altars at Fountains, and the cloister of the abbey, where she could never have set foot, seemed empty of meaning.

I walked home past her house. It was silent and shuttered, but at least it had not vanished like an enchanted castle, and I would be able to walk past it every day until I saw her again.

Or so I thought. I got back to find Brother Ambrose sitting downstairs, his ring of grey hair brushed into shiny curls and his face glowing with contentment.

"The fever has left me," he announced. "I feel utterly purified." He winked at Mistress Matilda. "And unspeakably hungry."

The next morning he set out with me to the abbey, taking

his usual way along the street to the guildhall. I padded after him, staring balefully up the alleyways that led to the market-place where I might have seen Marie, realising that I might never again have the chance to search for her.

For two weeks I staggered around in a fever of longing which grew stronger with every day that passed and left me struggling to hide the wanderings of my mind. When I sanded each finished page of parchment, I could hardly remember a word I had copied, and when one day a monk told us that Robert Bruce was still holding out in Berwick it took me several minutes to realise that this was bad news and that my face should be showing concern. No one remarked on it. For all they knew I was everything a follower of St. Bernard should be: deep in private prayer, lost in the silence of God.

In the end it was too much for me. One evening, when Mistress Matilda had gone home early leaving us in the middle of our supper, words came bubbling out of me.

"Brother Ambrose, have you ever loved a woman?"

"God forbid!" he spluttered, sending flakes of pastry tumbling down his cassock. "Only the Blessed Mary, Our Lady of Citeaux."

"Is it a great sin, then?"

"Not always," he said, dabbing his lips with his napkin. "St. Bernard wrote that unless a man has loved another human being he can never really know how to love God, and that loving is the art of all arts, so you might say that having been in love can help you become a monk. Mind you, it can easily be a monk's undoing. When I was a novice, the Abbot of Selby was deposed for it."

"For loving a woman?"

"Well, more for excess. One mistress was not enough for him, so he had two, and that was enough to outrage the Archbishop, who was no saint himself." He peered at me and gave an inquisitive pout. "What about you, Robert? Have you ever loved a woman?"

"Only My Lady Mary," I replied, thrilling at the truth and wincing at the blasphemy.

"Good boy," said Brother Ambrose. "You will indeed be ready to make your vows when we return to Fountains."

"When will that be?"

"Oh, we should have finished our work here in a month or so. I should say we will be home for Michaelmas." He arched his eyebrows. "Why the long face, Robert? Won't it please you to get back?"

"I was only thinking that I must not leave York without seeing the wonders of the Minster. Could we go there one day for Mass?"

"Bah," said Brother Ambrose. "You won't catch me setting foot in that den of thieves. You go if you wish. Sunday is the Feast of St. Mary Magdalene; the Archbishop himself should be preaching."

The Minster was crowded. All the burgesses of the city were there, and despite the heat their wives were showing off their best furred gowns and exchanging a week's gossip with such excitement that it was impossible to hear a word that was spoken by the Archbishop and canons at the high altar. Even the psalms of the choir could not silence them, but drifted upwards to make echoing clouds of unwanted music that floated beneath the high arched roof of the nave.

I elbowed my way through the crowd looking in every face, but there was no sign of Marie and after a while I gave up and raised my eyes to the glorious tall windows. The sunlight was on them, making the panes of stained glass flicker and glow like a tapestry of fire. I looked from picture to picture, recognising the stories of Christ and the saints, until my neck began to ache and I was forced to lower my gaze. It was then that I saw her.

She was lighting a candle in one of the chapels that lined the south aisle, and her back was towards me. As I began to push my way through to her she walked towards the doors, and I only caught up with her on the steps outside, where she had stopped to close her eyes and lift her face to the sun. She jumped with fright when I touched her on the shoulder, which meant that when she turned to me her eyes were startlingly wide.

"You," she said with relief. "I've forgotten your name."

"Brother Robert. I saw you inside and wanted to say I hope your mother was not too angry with you for talking to me."

She shook her head. "My mother is dead. That was Aunt Blanche, my father's sister. She hated my mother and she hates me. It was not your fault."

"Good, good." I swayed on my heels and grinned.

"Well," said Marie, "good day to you."

"Also . . ." I spoke quickly to stop her going.

"Yes?"

"It will not be long before I leave York. I wondered . . . I wondered if before I go you would come for a walk with me?"

She gave a hiccup of laughter. "A walk? Are white monks allowed to go walking with girls?"

I blushed and hung my head. "No," I confessed. "I am breaking the Rule even by talking to you."

Marie pointed to my hair. "You do not have the tonsure of a monk."

"I am still only a novice. When I return to the abbey I will make my vows."

"And then it is the cloister for the rest of your life?"

"Yes."

She looked at me a long moment, then leaned her head to one side. "Where would you be wanting to walk?"

"Anywhere."

"Very well," she said, and gave me a mischievous smile. "On St. Peter's Day there will be a fair on the meadow below the castle. You can be my escort. Meet me here when the bells ring the hour of Nones."

"Robert Bruce could not keep me away," I said gratefully.

"That is settled then. Till St. Peter's Day, Brother Robert." She curtseyed with lowered eyelids, then turned and swept away towards the gateway of the cathedral close.

When I got home Brother Ambrose met me with a questioning pout. "Well, what did you think of the citizens of York at worship?"

"You are right," I said. "It is a most unholy spectacle."

"Quite so," he said sternly. "You can take that smile off your face. It is nothing to laugh about."

July ended with days of cloudless sky. The city sweltered and the river shrank and grew sluggish in the heat. By noon of St. Peter's Day the older monks were dozing against the warm stone of the cloister arcade. Not long after that Brother Ambrose's head began to nod, and soon he was curled over his writing desk, snoring away and smiling like an angel. I closed my book and my inkwell and slipped out of the abbey.

The streets were almost deserted. The shops were shuttered and the cats were sleeping in the shade. I went straight to the Minster and walked down the cool aisles until the bells rang the hour of Nones. Stepping outside, I saw Marie walking towards me wearing a gown of dark russet, her hair plaited with ribbons. She was breathless and giggling.

"I thought I would never get free," she said. "Oh Brother Robert, you have saved my life today."

We set off through the streets. I waited tongue-tied while she recovered her breath and her giggles gave way to a grin.

"My aunt wanted me to spend the afternoon entertaining an ox," she explained.

"An ox?"

"A knight who looks like an ox. Blanche has made herself my guardian and set her heart on marrying me off before I come of age. She can make life unbearable." She made a sour face. "And that is my story. Now tell me yours. What made you become a novice if your real love in life is asking girls to walk with you?"

We were passing under the castle walls, through streets which were bustling with fair-goers. Looking up at the keep I saw the banner of Three Lions flying from the battlements.

"I would have been a knight," I said, and told her the story of my father's will. When I finished she was staring at me.

"And for the sake of that oath you are willing to make your vows and become a monk?" she asked incredulously.

I could not answer, so instead I asked a question. "What else can I do? Even if the Wheel of Fortune is the True Wheel I must find, what does that mean and how can I search for it?"

Marie shrugged. "If you like I can ask Eleazar David. My father called him the wisest man in York."

My words of thanks were drowned by shouting and a discordant fanfare on cheap trumpets. We had arrived at the fair.

Beneath the walls of the castle lay a tongue of meadow, bordered on either side by water and narrowing to a tip where the two rivers met. That afternoon it was packed with tents, booths, stalls and a multitude of people. We walked through the maze of it all like children in a dream, gaping at the acrobats and jugglers, laughing at two jesters who were mumming a story about a mean miller and a cunning priest, turning away from the sight of a bear being baited by some drunks. After years of silent cloister I was dizzy at the noise, but I wished it could last forever and I could spend my days in an enchanted pageant with Marie at my side and my ears filled with the music of flutes and timbrels.

Then we found we were being followed, by two young gallants in tight doublets and particoloured hose, who had jewels on their daggers and too much wine inside them. They came nearer and nearer until there was one on either side of us.

"I find this hard to believe," said the first, who had bloodshot blue eyes and curly hair. "The maid is even prettier than she looks from behind and yet she is wasting her company on a curd-faced monk."

"Who knows?" said the second, who was fair-haired and gawky. "She looks less than fifteen. Perhaps she is not strong enough for the company of men?"

Marie flushed crimson, then turned to me slowly and took my hand in hers. "Let's buy some fruit wafers and sit by the river," she said. "If these insects follow us we can push them in. It would be fun to find out if cockroaches can swim."

This only made them jeer louder. They followed us to the wafer stall, where there were too many women for them to get away with their games and they lost interest and drifted away. We took our wafers to the river bank and sat against a tree, looking across to the waterwheels of the mills that hung motionless above the sunken river.

"If your father had not made you swear that oath," said Marie, licking her fingers, "you would either be dead outside some border castle or you would have turned out like those two. I think he was a very wise man and loved you enough to save you."

"I wish I were free," I said. "I wish I were a knight and you were my lady, that I wore your love tokens into battle and came to you in a tent hung with silks from Baghdad and carpeted with flowers."

Marie slapped my wrist. "Stop it. You are living in dreams, Robert. The world is not like that."

I took her hand and kissed it. It tasted of fruit. "Why not?" I asked. "Today has been a dream come true, and I will remember it as long as I live."

She rolled her eyes and spent a long moment looking into

the river, then she reached into the neck of her gown and pulled a slim silver chain up over her head. From it there hung a silver ring set with a polished crystal of green jasper. Before I could say a word Marie had slipped the chain over my head.

"The one thing I can give you is a love token to remember it by," she said. "That is my mother's ring."

I was overcome. "You cannot give me this," I protested. "I have nothing to offer you in return."

She glared me into silence, then looked out at the river again. "You do not know that. I hate the young men my aunt shows me off to, and I am so rude to them that she curses me and calls me a spoilt little brat. You I like – all the more because you are monkish and different – and if I can give you something that makes you happy, then it makes me happy to do it."

All too soon it was the hours of Vespers, and we were standing on the corner of Marie's street smiling awkwardly at each other.

"I had better go home alone," she said, and untangled her fingers from mine. "If you can, come and say goodbye before you leave for the Abbey of Fountains."

I watched her walk quickly to her door and vanish inside the house. When I got back to St. Mary's Abbey, Brother Ambrose was still asleep.

Weeks went by as I worked in the library, but St. Peter's Day never left me. I had only to touch my chest and feel the silver ring with its green jasper hanging hidden beneath my cassock.

As September brought cooler days, the black monks in the cloister spoke of how time was running out for King Edward and his army at Berwick. Robert Bruce still held the fortress, and as autumn drew closer and the knights of England came no nearer to driving him out, it seemed more indestructible than ever. Archbishop William sang masses in the Minster, and Queen Isabelle herself left her halls in the castle to join him at the altar as he prayed for a victory to heal the realm.

Time was running out for me also. As the day of our return to Fountains drew closer, I spent every free moment reading, searching for the secret of the True Wheel that could set me free to live in the same world as Marie. I learnt a thousand and one things, but nowhere did I come across the one piece of knowledge that could save me from my vows; and once that oath to God was added to the oath I had given my father I would be caught between them, trapped forever like a speck of grit in a pane of glass.

As we bundled up our parchments at the end of our last day at St. Mary's, Brother Ambrose stopped to pat me on the shoulder.

"You can be proud of yourself, Robert. You have worked hard, and turned yourself into a scribe fit for a king."

"Is that an insult or a compliment?" I asked.

"A compliment. A good scribe is worth his weight in gold these days, and there will be scribes in the royal chancery with less than half your skill as a copyist."

His words kept me awake that night. The royal chancery was billeted in York Castle, where it would stay for the length of the King's border campaign. I imagined myself working there, living close to Marie, earning enough to ask her to be my wife . . .

In the morning our horses were ready long before we were. Brother Ambrose fussed lovingly over the packing of the books and insisted on doing it all himself. The delay gave me my chance.

"I would love one last glimpse of the windows of the Minster," I said wistfully.

He looked up from his packing and smiled. "Go on, then, but be quick. I want to be on the road by the hour of Terce."

Within minutes I was knocking breathlessly on Marie's

door. It was opened by her aunt, who wrinkled her nose as though I smelt.

"If you wish to see Marie, you will find her in the garden," she sneered, making the most beautiful words sound unpleasant.

The garden was sunk in morning shadow, and Marie was sitting beneath the fading leaves of the cherry tree. She jumped up at the sight of me, but when I reached her she was not smiling.

"Of course," she said softly. "You have come to say goodbye."

I took her hands in mine. "Do you remember all we said on St. Peter's Day?" I asked.

She grimaced. "That was in another lifetime. I am going to be married."

"Married?" I repeated numbly. "To whom?"

"A knight, the younger brother of the lord of Helmsley ..."

I let go of her hands and blundered backwards into a rose bush. "Married to a knight?" I repeated, my voice beginning to gargle like a blocked gutter. "What a prosperous match for a wine merchant's daughter."

"No Robert, please," she begged. "Not you ..."

"Well, I must be going," I said quickly. "Brother Ambrose is waiting with the horses." She shook her head and looked as though she were about to cry. "May God give you a long life," I mumbled, then I turned and ran for the door.

By the time I reached the market-place tears were streaming down my face so wantonly that I had to pull my hood forward and stumble through the streets with my eyes on the ground.

Brother Ambrose had finished packing and was talking to Mistress Matilda. He took one look at my eyes and his face filled with sympathy.

"My dear boy," he said, "you take me back thirty years to the day I had to say goodbye to the city of Paris."

We said farewell to Mistress Matilda and rode off, leading a donkey laden with our baskets of books, ducking beneath washing that had been hung out to dry on lines that stretched from house to house. As we turned into the great street and rode towards the gate-tower I tried and failed to remember the name of the city where some saint or other shook the dust from his feet as he left.

A man stepped out of the shadows of the gateway arch and barred our way with a pike. Brother Ambrose groaned and reached for his purse. "How much is the toll?" he asked wearily.

The man shook his head. "I've just had orders that no one is to leave."

"Preposterous," snorted Brother Ambrose. "Whose orders?"

A sergeant-at-arms came running down the steps from the wall. It was a cool morning but he was sweating. "My orders, Brother. Word has just come that the Scots have crossed the Tees. They are heading straight for the city."

In the same moment that he finished speaking, the bells of the Minster began to ring the alarm.

Chapter Six

THE WHITE BATTLE

WE HURRIED BACK to the house and threw ourselves into prayer. There was little else we could do.

Not long after Nones, Mistress Matilda came to tell us what was happening in the city. Queen Isabelle and her court had fled downriver by boat, and the richer merchants were leaving with as much as they could carry. In the castle the Lord Chancellor, Bishop John of Ely, was in council with Archbishop William and Sir Nicholas Flemming, the Lord Mayor of York.

"That's the last we'll see of them," muttered Brother Ambrose. "They'll sit there holding their council while the city burns around them. It will all be the way it was at Durham seven years ago."

"Just you put a little more trust in God," said Mistress Matilda. "Archbishop William has had it proclaimed that he will preach in the Minster at Vespers, and that he wants every man in the city to be there."

"I for one will never set foot in that temple of vanities," said Brother Ambrose.

"Indeed you will," said Mistress Matilda, "or you'll get no supper from me."

The Vesper bell was still ringing as we slipped through the door of the Minster. Brother Ambrose had pulled the hood of his cowl down as far as his nose, which struck me as an inadequate disguise when anyone who knew him would recognise his white-robed paunch. Neither of us were prepared for the scene we found inside. The nave and the transepts were crowded, but the crowd was quiet. The only sound was a wordless murmur of expectation as the first notes of the choir signalled the beginning of the service and the imminent arrival of the Archbishop. It seemed that Robert Bruce had done at a stroke what God had never done: reduced the citizens of York to silence.

In the hush, the songs and prayers of the Divine Office echoed around the heights of the Minster and swelled into a great furnace of sound. Even the roughest innkeepers were suddenly trying to impress God with their singing.

As Archbishop William climbed to the pulpit, the sound died away until all that could be heard was a child crying by one of the doors. Half baron, half prelate, the Archbishop drew himself up to his full height and towered above us like a giant.

"Let your hearts fill with faith," he cried, "and through faith you will do wonders. You think this is an hour of darkness, and you are wrong; it is an hour of light in which God has given us our chance to shine with His glory. You think that Robert Bruce is on his way to burn this city and foul the Minster of St. Peter, and you are wrong."

He leaned forward and pointed towards the north.

"Robert Bruce is penned in Berwick Castle by the army of our King," he cried triumphantly. "He knows his last hour has come, and that is why he flings at us a force of raiders led by the Black Douglas, in the hope we will be so filled with fear that we will call on the King to turn from Berwick and come to our help. Then Bruce could escape from the doom which at this very moment he feels tightening round his neck like a traitor's noose. And will we cry out in fear? Are we going to give Robert Bruce what he wants?"

"No," shouted one of the canons, and the cry was echoed by the crowd until people began to stamp their feet and the cry became a chant. Archbishop William nodded gravely and let the chant fill the Minster from end to end, then he held out his arms for silence and spoke on.

"You see how strong we are, and all we have to do is know it. So let us not hide behind our city walls while the Scots waste the land and burn our churches: let us hold high the banner of St. Peter and march out in faith to find them and crush them forever."

He hammered the pulpit with his fists, and the crowd gave a wild cheer and surged forward. I was caught and swept away from Brother Ambrose, and had to struggle to keep my feet in the crush of men shouting their throats raw. When I looked up I found I had been carried close to the pulpit, and staring up at Archbishop William I saw that his eyes were wide and his knuckles white on the pulpit rim, as though he were shocked and frightened by the force he had unleashed.

"Tonight!" he cried. "Gather here at sunset if you wish to follow St. Peter's banner. We will march by night, and tomorrow by the grace of God we will have victory over the Scots."

When the service was over I found Brother Ambrose and we elbowed our way outside. Once we were clear of the crowd, he walked with his lips pouting sombrely and his eyes on the ground and I took the risk of angering him by breaking silence in the open street.

"I will be marching with the Archbishop," I declared.

He nodded and kept his eyes on the ground. "I was afraid of that," he said, "but so will I."

At sunset we said Compline together in our chapel, then we shouldered the satchels of food Mistress Matilda had prepared for us and set off to join the army that was gathering in the cathedral close.

Archbishop William celebrated Mass on the Minster steps, then he raised the banner of St. Peter and we surged after him as he rode out into the streets, singing psalms while the women leaned from upper windows and called out blessings. It was like the stories they tell of the first crusade. With the Archbishop and Sir Nicholas Flemming rode several hundred horsemen, followed by a multitude in which priests, monks, and choirboys rubbed shoulders with townspeople and peasants. Brother Ambrose and I walked with them, wishing we had taken our horses, and behind us rumbled bullock-carts stacked with weapons from every rafter and store-chest in the city.

Once beyond the city walls and out among the forests and fields of the Vale of York, the singing died away and we settled down to the grind of the march. Word went round that our goal was Boroughbridge, where the Archbishop planned to hold the crossing of the Eure against the Scots, but towards dawn we saw a dull red glow to the north, a glow made by flames rising high off the ground, and as the sky grew lighter we saw smoke hanging over the land.

The Scots had reached Boroughbridge before us.

In the cold light of dawn the army that had looked so invincible in the torchlit night turned into a ragged host of priests and beggars. Half of us looked worn out by the march; few of us looked like soldiers. Even the horsemen were mostly canons of the Minster and their servants. The few men-at-arms were moving among the host giving out weapons, and one of them handed me a long pike with a cruel point and a curved blade.

"I have never used one," I protested.

"There's no great craft to it," he said wearily. "If a footman comes at you, jab him in the stomach and lift him off his feet. If it's a rider, pike him in the armpit and lift him off his horse."

I nodded and walked on. The pike was so heavy that even carrying it over my shoulder made my arms ache.

Soon after that we came into Boroughbridge. The Scots

had vanished, leaving behind them a scene out of hell. The houses were still burning. Women and children lay dead outside their doorways. Men had been hung from trees and mutilated. The air was so full of the stink of burning that it was hard to breathe.

"May God receive their souls," said Brother Ambrose. He saw the horror in my face and put his arm around me. "Poor Robert," he said. "What did you expect? Deeds of chivalry?"

Our march ground to a halt in the desolate remains of the market-place, where flasks of wine were passed round while riders were sent out to scout for the tracks of the Scots. When they returned, the Archbishop and Sir Nicholas Flemming held a council, at the end of which the Archbishop was lifted, pale and haggard, onto the stump of the broken market cross to speak to us.

"You can all see the evil we are fighting," he said. "The Scots have returned to the north bank of the river and must be hoping to follow it down towards York. The hour of our trial is close at hand."

After leading us in prayer he led us over the long wooden bridge to the far riverbank, and we were grateful to follow if only to leave the smoking town behind us. The Scottish tracks led east through lush meadows, and at the Archbishop's command we began singing the psalms of Prime.

Away to our left was a field with three haystacks and beyond it the forest fringe, and as we passed the field the haystacks caught fire. Thick yellow smoke blew straight into our faces, and with it came the sound of weird cries and hunting horns, and then of hoofbeats. Through the swirling smoke we saw riders on shaggy stunted horses, galloping towards us and yelling like the demons of hell. One of them, wearing a red cloak and waving an axe, seemed to be riding straight at me.

I swung my pike to point it at him and tried to hold it

steady, but the Scot nimbly passed the axe to his other hand and grabbed the pike-shaft below the blade, jerking it upwards to that the butt hit me under the chin and knocked me head over heels to land on my stomach with a thud that kicked the breath out of me. Then he swept on by and someone behind me screamed. Other horsemen came thundering by, and as the hoofbeats and screaming filled my ears I buried my face in the grass and lay there shaking.

It was only when the hoofbeats and screams came from further away that I found the courage to lift my head and open my eyes. The battle had become a strange dance of shadows in the coiling smoke, and the ground was littered with bodies in every vestment of the church. I found Brother Ambrose lying on his face and breathing heavily, and when I rolled him over I saw a gash in his stomach through a blood-soaked tear in his cassock.

"My dear boy," he panted. "What will Abbot Walter say?"

"Can you crawl?" I asked.

"I may never again do anything else," he replied, rolling over with a grunt.

We began to crawl across the meadows in the opposite direction to the sounds of battle, dropping to the ground whenever horsemen came near, pressing ourselves flat against the dead. Through the smoke I made out a shape that looked big enough to hide behind. It turned out to be one of the bullock-carts, and as I dragged Brother Ambrose into its shelter, I came face to face with someone else who was hiding there – the curly-haired cockroach who had jeered at Marie and me at the fair. We stared at each other, then he gave me a nod of recognition.

"Are you looking for a way out of this?" he asked.

"Is there one?"

"The river. If we can reach it the current will carry us away." He glanced at Brother Ambrose, who was clutching his stomach and breathing in gulps. "We can carry him," he added.

Together we lifted Brother Ambrose to his feet and stumbled the twenty or so yards to the riverbank. When we reached the brink we stopped and gaped. The river ran fast and deep, but it was a long way below us: the heavy rains and floods of the previous summers had cut away the bank to leave us perched on the lip of a ten foot cliff of sheer mud. As we stood there dithering, the smoke began to thin and we heard hoofbeats hammering towards us.

We jumped; or rather, we took a step forward into thin air and plunged down into the water, dragging Brother Ambrose with us. The river folded over us like a shroud, pulling us down to the bottom where we sank up to our ankles in mud, then swirling us up to the surface again with such speed that we lost hold of each other. As soon as our heads were in the air and we could see what we were doing, the cockroach and I grabbed Brother Ambrose. The three of us promptly sank like a stone, and performed a kind of staggering dance along the river bed before we were able to push ourselves up and break the surface.

"Kick with your . . . " spluttered the man from the fair, his mouth filling with water as we went under again. I kicked and found that my legs slurred feebly through the water as though a spell had been laid on them, while my cassock had turned as heavy as lead and was dragging at my knees; but sure enough it kept us afloat, and the current was carrying us away.

Within moments we were passing a narrow tip of land formed by another river flowing into the Eure, and once we were downstream of it, I had a view of the whole battlefield. The haystacks had burned to the ground and the smoke was clearing. The scattered English were being hunted down by the Scottish riders, being herded like sheep onto the spit where the rivers met, and slaughtered in swathes. They had no room to move, and when they tried to escape by plunging into the river they fell over and on top of each other. I saw people drowning, while above them on the bank the Scots yelled themselves hoarse as they went about their killing.

Then the current swept us around the bend and out of sight of the battle, where the splashes and gasps of our desperate paddling were the only strange sounds in a quiet world of sunlight and birdsong.

The river widened and we came to a place where the banks were low and there was a shallow ford where we dragged ourselves out onto the east bank and set off at once along a lane that led into the forest. The water seemed to have sucked all our strength away, and we swayed on our feet like drunkards. Brother Ambrose's face had set into a grey and expressionless mask, but he kept on his feet and trudged on with his hand on my shoulder.

After an eternity we reached a road where carts packed with peasants and their families were heading for the safety of the city walls. I remember heaving Brother Ambrose up into the back of a cart which held two frightened children and a ginger cat, and stretching out beside him to lie with my legs dangling over the road and swinging wildly with each turn of the wheels.

When I awoke I was in a long room with a roof of vaulted stone, and I thought for a moment that I was back in the Abbey of Fountains. Twilight was pouring through arched windows and turning the stone the colour of cider.

Sitting up I saw nuns bustling to and fro, and that I was on one of many beds that lined the room. One of the sisters saw me stretching and shivering; she hurried out of the room and returned with my cassock, giving me a motherly smile as she helped me pull it over my head.

"You came to us looking dead, and you will leave us as full of life as the day you were born," she said happily. "We have dried your cassock in our kitchen, but that is all the healing need from us."

"Where am I?" I asked.

"Safe in the city, in the Hospice of St. Leonard."

I looked at the empty beds around me. "Have any others escaped?" I asked.

She patted my hand. "We will soon know. Carts have been sent out to bring back the wounded."

"No. No one must leave the city," I said quickly. "All they will find are Scots. The Scots are everywhere."

"The word is that Lord Douglas and his men have ridden west," said the nun, "towards Knaresborough and the hills. York has been spared."

"Spared?" I repeated dimly.

"Indeed," she said firmly. "So you must thank Our Lady Mary for protecting you. In your sleep you called her name."

My hands went to my chest. The ring was still there, hanging on its chain of silver. The sister watched me with raised eyebrows.

"Or perhaps the thanks should go to your ring?" she said. "Is it magical?"

"It was," I said. "No, it still is." My gaze went round the beds again. "How is Brother Ambrose?" I asked.

She laughed and patted her stomach. "He also was fortunate. The weapon struck him in the best protected part of his body."

I found him in a bed in the upper hall of the hospice, propped up with pillows and with his hands folded over his pierced paunch.

"They say it will be seven days before they let me walk out of here," he told me in an irate whisper, "and another seven after that before I am fit to ride. By the time we get back, the Martinmas account will be piling up into a heap big enough to bury us."

"It may be weeks before the country is free of the Scots," I said, but I was thinking of the ring and telling myself I had no right to be wearing it.

Brother Ambrose sighed philosophically. "Ah well, when one door closes another one opens. Two weeks should just give you time to copy another of the treasures in the library of St. Mary's."

When I left the hospice it was past the hour of Vespers and the twilight was fading over the city. Brother Ambrose had given me our purse, so I bought a bowl of spiced broth in a tavern near the guildhall. From the gossip of the drinkers, I learnt that Sir Nicholas Flemming was among the dead and that Archbishop William had only escaped by the skin of his teeth. There was much joking about how the battle had rid the city of some unwanted priests and of the unholy scramble there would be for the livings that had fallen vacant.

Marie's house was dark save for lamplit windows in the upper chamber, and it was a while before I heard footsteps coming to answer my knocking. The door was opened by Aunt Blanche, who greeted me with a curling smile of utter contempt.

"If it's Marie you want you won't find her here," she said drily.

Straining every nerve to keep my face blank, I met her gaze with the devotional mask of a monk. "May I ask when she will return? She has undertaken a transaction with Eleazar David on behalf of my abbey."

"She will not be returning," said Aunt Blanche, lingering over each word as though it were a dish to be savoured. "She was married this morning, and at noon she left the city with her husband."

"Married?" I repeated. "Today of all days she was married?"

"Why ever not?" asked Aunt Blanche. "We could not allow the Scots to spoil our careful arrangements, and her husband is a knight, well able to escort her safely to her new home."

Somehow I carved a smile into my face. "What joyous news," I exclaimed. "My brothers and I will pray for her happiness. Who is the good man whose name we must add to our prayers?"

"Sir Girald de Ros. You may have seen his coat-of-arms in the windows of Holy Trinity, the church where the wedding was celebrated."

I only had to close my eyes to see it – a strange device like six gourds hanging from three sticks. "He is the husband of her choice?" I asked incredulously.

"The husband of my choice," Aunt Blanche corrected me. "As her guardian it was for me to decide what was best for her."

The glow of triumph in her face was too much for me. "You evil crone," I said bitterly. "Girald de Ros is a murderer."

She gave me a withering glare. "Run along, little monk, or I'll call the men of the watch and have you kicked down the gutters."

And with that she shut the door on me.

I wandered off down the dark streets, feeling the ring hanging cold against my chest, and I forget where I walked but eventually I came to the Minster. It was open and candle-lit and women were keeping a vigil at the tomb of St. William, praying for sons and husbands who were probably staring sightlessly up at the stars from the meadows by the Eure. I walked along the south aisle, looking for the chapel where I once caught sight of Marie lighting a candle.

It was the Chapel of St. Catherine, the patron saint of unmarried girls, and above the altar was a tapestry showing Catherine's martyrdom on the wheel. I put two pence into the offerings box and lit two tall candles.

"Holy Catherine," I whispered. "One is for me and the other is for Marie. Help me find her."

Chapter Seven

THE FOREST OF GALTRES

When Mistress Matilda came to open the abbey house in the morning she found me slumped on the doorstep. She took me inside, fed me as I told her the story of the battle, then bundled me upstairs to bed.

"No copying manuscripts today," she said. "Sleep is what you need. I'll go and pamper Brother Ambrose."

It was well after Nones when I awoke, and the house was empty. I drank some milk, slipped my cowl over my shoulders and pulled up the hood, then ducked through the doorway and out into the city.

The streets were packed and the shops full of people; it was as if the Scots had been no more than a dream. I made my way to the street of the guildhall, along one side of which the houses of what had once been the Jewish quarter stretched down to the river. An urchin girl was selling eggs from two baskets filled with straw, and for a farthing she told me the way to the house of Eleazar David. It lay down a stinking alley where two old men were gutting herrings on a length of sacking, and I knew when I reached a door marked by a circle of yellow paint that I had come to the house of a Jew.

My knock was answered by an old man with close-cropped silvery hair and the palest of blue eyes. "Eleazar David?" I asked, and when he nodded I named myself. He smiled when I named the Abbey of Fountains.

He led me across a narrow courtyard where a dark-eyed girl was washing linen and up a wooden stairway to a low-rafted room whose windows overlooked the river. In one corner was a table with a chequered cloth and an iron casket on it, but all around the other walls were book-chests on which manuscripts of every size and colour were rolled or piled. Eleazar offered me a stool and settled himself into a finely-carved armchair.

"I have been doing business with the Abbey of Fountains for twenty-seven years," he said, "and you are the first of its monks I have seen with my own eyes. I was wondering how you would break the silence that followed Jocelin's death." He raised his hand to stop my mumbled apology. "No, no, I do not say it in bitterness. Tell me what I can do for you. Has Brother Ambrose sent you with an order for more books?"

I shook my head. "No one from the abbey knows I am here. I came to ask you how I can find Marie."

Eleazar frowned. "Why do you wish to?"

"I have to speak to her."

"Well, she spoke of you to me," he said. "Twice she spoke warmly, and then the last time I saw her she spoke coldly, as though she had no wish ever to see you again."

I squirmed with shame. "That is why I have to speak to her," I said, pleading with my eyes.

He shrugged and looked out onto the river. "You have left it rather late. Her aunt has put her where you and I can never reach her. Girald de Ros is a bad man with powerful friends. She is his property now, and he is the kind of man who kills people who trespass on his property."

"I wanted to help her run away," I said weakly.

"So did I," said Eleazar, "but there was no time. Her aunt only told her two days before the wedding." He made a fluttery gesture with his hands. "Marie came to me. She begged me to hide her until there was the chance of a passage on a ship bound for Aquitaine. What could I say? There is no ship until Michaelmas. Her aunt would have gone to the mayor and told him that a Jew had stolen a Christian maiden; I would have been lynched with my children beside me and Marie would still have had to marry de Ros."

For a long moment we sat staringly bleakly at one another. A hundred songs about knights riding to the rescue laughed at me from the back of my mind.

"You say there is a ship at Michaelmas?" I asked. "In eight days' time?"

"Why talk about it?"

I sat forward. "If I find Marie and bring her back to York, and hide her in a house owned by the abbey until it is time for the ship to leave, would you pay for her passage to Aquitaine?"

His answer was to lift his hands in despair. "How old are you?" he asked.

"Seventeen."

"Then it is time you learnt to accept powerlessness. If you don't you will not live to grow old."

"But I know what it is to be powerless," I all but shouted at him. "I know what it is to do nothing but pray. I know what it is to run away from a battle. All I know now is that if I run away from Marie I will never have peace for the rest of my life."

Eleazar leaned forward and put his hands on mine. "I do not doubt you," he said gently. He walked over to one of the book-chests and rummaged in it, returning with a thin scroll of goatskin which he unrolled and spread on my lap. It was a map of the land from York eastwards to the sea on which rivers, towns, and abbeys were marked in red and green ink.

"I had this made two years ago for a family who intended to make a pilgrimage to the Shrine of St. Hilda at Whitby. Two of them died in the second winter of the famine and the journey was never made. Here is Helmsley, where Girald de Ros has his castle; it cannot be more than two days from

York." He sat back and folded his arms. "Even to talk like this is mad when she is in the hands of de Ros. If you knew the kind of creature he is . . ."

"I know," I cut in. "When I was twelve, I saw him kill a man."

Eleazar threw up his hands again. "What is the use? I am singing to the deaf."

"But if I succeed," I said, "will you do the rest?"

"I will pay her passage, and I have friends in Bordeaux who will look after her," he replied. "If ever it comes to that."

"It will," I promised.

As I left the house he asked me to wait a moment, and darted into a small room in one of the corners of the courtyard. He returned with a small leather pouch tied with a thong, which he thrust into my hand.

"Crushed seeds of henbane and black poppy," he explained. "Mix it into a flagon of wine in the evening and whoever drinks from it will sleep like the dead for the night. God go with you, Brother Robert."

I thanked him and pushed the pouch and the map up my sleeve, and had hardly taken two steps into the street when he called me back.

"I almost forgot," he said. "Marie told me of your quest for something called the True Wheel, and asked if in my reading or my travels I had learnt the meaning of it."

"Yes?" I said eagerly.

"I am sorry. I have never heard of it before in my life."

I spent the evening lying in bed, poring over the map and trying to guess which would be the best of the three roads that led to Helmsley. All of them passed through the Forest of Galtres, a name I rolled over my tongue and smiled at; it seemed the perfect place to hide from Girald de Ros, just as Tristan and Iseult once vanished into the wildwood to escape King Mark of Cornwall.

Late that evening when I had the house to myself, I went downstairs and wrote a letter for Mistress Matilda to give to Brother Ambrose. I wrote that I had received a message from my sister at Richmond who begged me to go to her at once. It was in my mind that if all went well I would soon have a sister to show them.

When the letter was finished I packed a saddlebag with food, then went back to bed and spent the night listening to the rain pattering on the shutters.

The dawn was sunless and drab under a fleece of dull cloud. Padding down the wet alley I called the stable-boy down from his hayloft to saddle my horse, and rode off through the empty streets to be the first person out of the city when the gates were opened at the hour of Prime.

I chose the northernmost of the three roads that wound east to Helmsley, the one that would take me by way of the Bernardine abbey at Byland where I hoped to spend the night. All morning I rode through stretches of forest and small villages where pigs and cattle grazed on the stubble of the harvested fields, and towards noon I came in sight of the castle of Sheriff Hutton. It was market-day in the village that clustered in the shelter of the battlements, and I stopped to buy fodder for my horse and a goat's milk cheese for myself. To keep out the cold I went into a tavern and drank two pints of cider. Either my legs were numb from the ride or the cider was stronger than the abbey brew, but for one reason or another I needed three attempts before I succeeded in clambering back onto my horse.

Beyond Sheriff Hutton the villages were fewer and the Forest of Galtres took over the land. The trees were older and taller, twisting upwards to overhang the road and decked out in their autumn leaf colours of gold, rust, and amber. It was a place to make the head swirl with cidery thoughts, and I told myself that no knight had ever travelled the world on so noble a quest as mine. I remembered the songs of the troubadours and began singing at the top of my voice.

All of a sudden I saw a black shape hovering above me, and it became a man dropping out of a tree. He landed on my shoulders and we cartwheeled off the horse into the mud. A second man ran out of the woods and grabbed my horse by its bridle, while my attacker pulled me to my feet and slammed me against the trunk of a tree. One of his teeth was blue, and he had a long dark knife which he levelled under my chin so that the point pricked against my throat.

"Money," he whispered.

"In the saddlebag," I croaked.

"Good," he said, and nodded to the second man who began searching for it. "You'd better not be lying," said the man with the knife. "I hate white monks. I hate the way they grow fat on their granges while the forest people starve, and I've been wanting to kill one for a long time."

With his free hand he began to untie the thongs of my belt-pouch, but in that instant a man in the long grey robes of a Franciscan friar stepped out of the trees behind him.

"Stand away," he commanded the robbers.

The man with the knife cursed and ran at the Franciscan, who reached into his robes and drew out a long crusader's sword, which curved through the air and cleaved the robber's head from his shoulders. The second brigand leapt onto my horse and galloped away down the road. I watched the severed head with its blue tooth roll through the mud and drop face down into a wheel-rut.

The Franciscan cleaned his sword on the robber's jerkin and stared at me with two cold eyes which froze my words of thanks to my lips. He had hair which had once been golden and was brindled to grey, a gaunt face marked by an old scar that creased his right cheek from chin to cheekbone, and there was something about him which was ten times more frightening than the robber with the blue tooth.

"What in God's name are you doing here alone?" he snapped. "Where do you think you are? The Garden of Delights?"

"I'm on a pilgrimage," I spluttered. "To Whitby . . . to the Shrine of St. Hilda."

"A pilgrim?" he repeated in a puzzled voice which had lost its harshness, then he shook his head and gave a dry laugh. "Then I must help you," he said. "Where were you heading before you lost your horse and your money?"

"The Abbey of Byland."

"I can get you there by nightfall," he said. "Come with me."

He led me a short distance into the trees to where a stream curled through the forest. A large white horse was grazing beside it, so big-boned that in its youth it must have been a charger fit for a knight, and close by on the bank its owner's possessions were strewn around the smoking embers of a fire.

"You woke me with your singing," said the Franciscan, offering me a gourd of wine. "How does a white monk come to be singing songs like that?"

"When I was a boy I lived in Richmond Castle," I answered, surprised by the ornateness of the saddle he was lifting onto the horse's back and buckling into place. "How did you become a friar?" I asked.

"That is between me and God," he said darkly as he swung himself up into the saddle. "I thought white monks were meant to follow a vow of silence?"

He heaved me up to sit behind him and we cantered through the trees and out onto the road. I hung on silently, thanking the angels that the map and Eleazar's potion were still safe in my belt-pouch but wishing they would tell me how to get to Helmsley with no horse and no money.

The day was drawing in when we came in sight of low brackened hills and the forest gave way to fields and orchards which bore the stamp of grangeland. In the distance I saw the high roofs and brown walls of the Abbey of Byland. The Franciscan reined to a halt.

"This is where we part," he said.

I slid to the ground and tried to find the words to thank him.

"You can thank me," he replied, "by telling no one you met me."

Peering up at the hard lines of his face I realised that he wore his stare like a mask.

"Are you an outlaw?" I asked.

"That also is between me and God," he said; and with that he turned and rode away into the forest.

The arrival at dusk of an unknown brother was strange enough to make the monks of Byland cluster round and ogle me as though I had walked all the way from Jerusalem. Abbot Aylmer himself came hurrying along the cloister to listen to my story, and I told them the whole pack of lies.

"This pilgrimage," asked the Abbot, "why are you making it?"

"For Brother Ambrose," I answered. "He is my teacher and gravely ill in St. Leonard's Hospice. I wish to pray to St. Hilda for his cure."

The brothers believed every word, and they could not have been kinder. They led me to the refectory to share their supper of vegetable stew and elderberry pancakes; they heated water for me to bathe; and they gave me a bed in their own dormitory. In the morning I joined them in their choir, and when I made to leave after Mass they pressed me to stay with them as they filed into the chapter house.

"We have all been moved by Brother Robert and his pilgrimage," said Abbot Aylmer, and the assembled monks nodded in agreement. "Let us ask him to accept a gift of three marks with which to buy a horse and his food for the journey, and ask him in return to pray for our souls at the Shrine of St. Hilda."

So they pressed a purse into my hand and came to the abbey gates to wave me on my way, and they were so shining in their love and brotherhood that I wished the ground would open up and swallow me for my lies.

I walked east over the moors, with the wind at my back and the clouds blowing ahead of me, and knew by midday that I could be in Helmsley by nightfall. But just as the knights on quests have visions of enchanted castles, so that afternoon I came down into a wooded valley and crossed a packhorse bridge of arched stones where my eyes strayed upstream and I first caught sight of the Abbey of Rievaulx.

It stood on the slope of the valley side, and as if to make up for being on so cramped a perch, it soared upwards in walls and arches of creamy-white stone. To see it was to feel the beginnings of our Order, for this was where the first monks sent north by St. Bernard made their home, the monks who in passing through York had inspired the discontented brothers of St. Mary's to leave and found the Abbey of Fountains. Byland and Jervaulx were no more than children; Rievaulx was the mother, the queen of them all. I could not bring myself to walk on by. I turned off the Helmsley road and hurried towards the white buildings. Without realising it, I had become a pilgrim.

The guest-master was called Brother Jacob, and had travelled all the way from Flanders to make his vows at Rievaulx. He led me proudly into the church, through the stark old nave which echoed the austere voice of St. Bernard, and on into the new presbytery which rose up in an intricate lattice of arches, columns and windows which took my breath away.

"I thought the Chapel of Nine Altars at Fountains was the most glorious place on earth," I whispered, "but now I am not so sure."

"Like you," said Brother Jacob, "we went into debt to build this."

When he said 'we' he meant the Rievaulx monks of fifty years earlier, but standing there we were part of a living body that had grown through countless generations of men, of something far older than Edward of Caernarvon and his blighted wars. Lifting my eyes to the six tall windows above the altar I felt the power of the Rule I was betraying, but it was too late to tell the truth. A handful of miles beyond those windows was Helmsley Castle, and Marie.

At dawn the next morning, I shut myself in the abbey library and burrowed into the chronicles to learn all I could of the land around. I was in there for hours, while the monks on the other side of the wall sang their way through the Divine Office from Prime to Mass, and as they were filing into the chapter house I said my farewells and made off towards a nearby hamlet where they had told me there was a smith called Alun who hired out his horses.

He was a small man with a lopsided grin and a bald head that looked as though the hair had been scorched off by the heat of the forge, and he put down the threshing-hook he was tempering to hear what I wanted.

"Not today," he answered. "I have three mares and they're hired out till sunset. Tomorrow and any day after you can have any one o'them. Where do you want to go?"

"Helmsley."

"Helmsley?" he repeated with a jeering laugh. "Why hire a horse to go to Helmsley? Set off now on your legs and you'll be there by noon."

"So I will," I said, "But I still need two horses at first light tomorrow for a journey to York."

"York?" he repeated, this time with a shake of the head and a rub of the chin. "That's a long way."

"No it is not," I protested. "One and a half day's riding

to get there, and I'll pay someone to ride the horses back to you."

"Hmmm," he said and studied a scab on his wrist.

"I will pay you half a mark for two mares for three days."

"Will you now?" he asked, brightening back into a grin. "You must want them a lot if you'll pay that. In a hurry, are you?"

I was beginning to fluster. "I have to escort my sister to see our dying mother," I said solemnly.

Alun roared with laughter. "Ah, you mean it's a maiden you're running away with? I'll be glad to hire my horses for so noble a purpose."

I must have turned as pale as a bowl of curds, for he laughed even harder; but he did make the bargain.

"First light tomorrow, then, I'll have the mares waiting for you. The secret is safe with me."

Fleeing down the valley I tried to calm myself by memorising every feature of the road so as to know it in darkness.

Just as the map had told me it would, the valley grew wider and the hills fell away into the flat wooded vastness of the Vale of Pickering. Jutting above the trees ahead of me were the pale stone turrets of Helmsley Castle.

A narrow bridge led me across a wide ditch to a deserted stone gateway from the sides of which rickety wooden palisades stretched around the top of the inner bank. I smiled at the simplicity of it and walked through, only to be stopped in my tracks by the sight of what lay beyond. Another bridge ran across a second, deeper ditch, the bottom of which was full of stagnant water and sewage, and on its inner bank rose high stone ramparts with crenellated walkways and a drawbridge gateway with guard towers on either side of it. On the top of one of the towers was what looked like a pumpkin on a pole, but turned out on closer scrutiny to be a human head, rather the worse for wear of weather, which had probably belonged to a horse thief or someone of the sort.

Either the drawbridge was rickety or my legs were shaking as I crossed it. The brawny guard in the gateway gave me a cheery smile.

"Good day to you, Brother. You have business with us?"

"Indeed I have," I said, "with Lord de Ros himself."

The guard waved me past.

Chapter Eight

THE AIR OF THE NIGHT

ONCE THROUGH the gateway I walked into a scene that was more like a stone quarry than a castle yard. The ground was littered with freshly-cut blocks of limestone. Wooden scaffolding was set against the inside of the curtain wall, on which workmen were knocking down the old ramparts and building new, taller battlements. A new doorway had been cut high in the side of the keep, and leaning in its archway as he watched the workmen was Girald de Ros.

I was staring up at him wondering what to do next when a stout man in a furred gown came up to me.

"I am Ralph the steward," he announced. "Who might you be?"

"Brother Robert from the Abbey of Fountains," I replied, summoning up a voice of monkish calm. "I wish to speak with Lord Girald de Ros."

The steward smiled fleetingly. "Sir Girald is not the Lord de Ros, though you might be forgiven for thinking he is. Follow me."

He led me into the keep and up a wide spiral staircase.

"Who, then, is the Lord de Ros?" I asked. "I thought that was the title of the master of Helmsley?"

"So it is," said the steward, "and the title belongs to Lord William, Sir Girald's elder brother."

We passed through a dusty and newly-floored chamber and came to the doorway onto the ramparts in which Girald was still leaning. He made a fine figure of a man, tall with a neatly-clipped brown beard and hawklike blue eyes, and I cringed at the thought of how good he must look to Marie. The steward named me to him and left us.

"From the Abbey of Fountains," repeated Girald in a voice lazy with disinterest. "Whatever brings you to me?"

"My brothers and I are cruelly oppressed," I began. "The Earl of Lancaster wishes to take our two oldest granges from us, and I have been sent to ask your help, to beg you to ask him to respect our lands and leave us in peace."

His eyebrows arched upwards in surprise. "But Thomas is my feudal lord, and why should I care a fig about your granges?"

I took a deep breath and poured out all I had learnt in the library at Rievaulx. "Because it was your ancestor Walter l'Espec who granted the lands of Rievaulx to our Order and first brought the monks of St. Bernard to the North. Your family has always had a high place in our prayers, and you are the knight we turn to in our hour of need."

"Well you can turn somewhere else," said Girald. "Tell your brothers they are rich enough to protect themselves, and if you think that will upset them too much, tell them that there isn't a knight in England who can protect them from Earl Thomas. I suggest you give him what he wants and get into his favour."

I did my best to look shaken. "If that is your lordship's answer," I mumbled, "then my journey has been in vain."

"That is my answer," said Girald. I took a risk and turned to go, looking as mournful as a wet sheep. "Wait," he said. "It is almost the hour of dinner. Eat in my hall before you go. Ralph the steward will find you a place."

"I thank your lordship. . ." I began.

He nodded dismissively, spat into the moat and walked off along the rampart.

The hall was a long upper chamber whose high glazed

windows looked out through the castle walls to the fields beyond, and walking into it, I seemed to step back five years to the hall of Richmond Castle with its view over the valley of the Swale. The steward placed me at a trestle table packed with men-at-arms who nudged each other and sniggered at the sight of my robes.

"You're the first servant of God to come to Helmsley in a long while," said a hook-nosed man in a greasy leather jerkin. "Girald must be losing his grip."

I shivered with memories: it was the archer who had murdered the Templar. "Does the castle have no chaplain?" I asked.

"Not these days," said the archer. "One of the black canons of Kirkham comes over at Easter and Pentecost, but the rest of the year we use the chapel for storing grain."

He fell silent as a door opened in the corner of the hall and a man and a woman stepped through from the adjoining tower. The man was like Girald, only older, with a dark doublet and a stoop to his shoulders; the woman carried herself like a queen but was as thin as a piece of rope. Behind them walked a sickly boy of about seven, and behind him swaggered Girald, with Marie at his side. Her face was pale and lifeless, and she walked like a wraith, her eyes to the ground. As soon as the procession had seated itself at the high table the servers came scurrying up the stairs and the meal began.

The main dish was a mawmeny of spiced minced chicken which I had to refuse, contenting myself with a double helping of frizzled beans. As often as I dared I turned my head and gazed at Marie. She sat stiffly beside Girald, eating from the same trencher and drinking from the same goblet, and all the while looking only at her hands as if she were willing everything else in the hall to disappear. Girald was playfully gallant and offered her choice morsels with his fingers; she accepted them dutifully, the muscles of her throat twitching as though at each mouthful she were swallowing a stone.

"Beautiful, is she not?" said the archer, making me blush and look back at my plate. "No, no, gaze as much as you like," he said. "We all do."

"She looks unhappy," I said.

"Aye, she's a moody little piece," agreed the archer. "She never says a word to anyone." He leaned closer with a foxy smile. "That is why Girald enjoys taunting her. If she adored him and doted on his every word, he wouldn't be able to stand the sight of her."

"Why in God's name did he marry her?" I asked, in a voice that was none too steady.

The archer rubbed his fingers together. "Loot. Her father was a rich wine merchant. You must have seen all the building going on in the castle? Well, her dowry is paying for it."

I was well and truly puzzled. "But why? Why should Sir Girald spend his wife's dowry on his brother's castle? Why not use it to build a castle of his own?"

The archer leaned even closer. "Does Lord William look healthy to you? Does his son and heir look built for a long life? One more famine like we had two years ago and who would be surprised if they died? That would make Girald the lord of Helmsley."

"Even to think like that is evil," I protested. The archer shrugged and poured himself more wine, and I guessed that he and most of the men-at-arms in the hall were biding their time, following Girald for his Fortune in the same way that Girald followed Thomas of Lancaster. In that moment I saw the Wheel of Fortune as a disease, the symptom of which was greed and the fever of which was the evil that hung in the air of Helmsley. It turned Marie into nothing more than a girl who was useful for her money and useless as soon as it was spent, unless Girald also wanted sons ... The dessert was a dish of dates and peeled nuts in jelly. I pushed mine away.

The meal ended when the noble folk at the high table rose and walked towards the doorway of their private chambers in the west tower. Springing to my feet, I hurried over to bow in front of Girald and block his way, and I heard Marie catch her breath as she recognised me.

"No more pleading," warned Girald. "It tires me."

"As your lordship pleases," I said humbly. "I wish only to ask if I may recite the office of Nones in the chapel before I leave?"

"By all means," he said. "I'm sure it does the place good to be used every now and then. Ralph will unlock it for you."

"Brother Monk," said Marie, "would you hear my confession?"

I kept my eyes firmly on the ground. "If I can be of any service to God and to your ladyship . . . "

"What have you got to confess?" cut in Girald with a sneer. He signalled to me to move out of the way. "You will await Lady Marie in the chapel," he commanded, and with that he squeezed her arm and swept her out of the hall.

Ralph the steward swung open the heavy doors of the chapel and left me to find my own way in past piled sacks of grain and barrels of salted meat. Pigeons were nesting on the high rafters and their droppings spattered the walls and floor, but the building itself had a stillness which was like balm after the smells and clatter of the hall. The autumn sun shone as pale as Marie through the smoky glass of the traceried windows.

The chapel could not have been more than seventy years old, but it seemed to belong to another world – the age of the crusades and the Knights Templar, when men were strong in their faith and Christendom stretched from Jerusalem to Iceland – a lost world that had given way to one where the Scots and the English prayed to the same God before they killed each other. I knelt down on the dusty steps and tried to clear my mind with prayer.

Soft footsteps crossed the stone floor behind me and I rose to find Marie reaching out her hands for mine. The paleness of her face made her eyes greener than ever, but there were red sores at the corners of her mouth.

"Robert, what are you doing here?" she asked.

"I had to see you, to plead with you to forgive me for all I said that last day in York."

She gave a cracked laugh and attempted a smile. "You came all this way to ask me that?"

"And to ask you to take one more walk with me," I said, and raised her hand to my lips. "There will be horses waiting for us at daybreak at Rievaulx. We can ride to York, where I will hide you until Michaelmas when a ship sails for Aquitaine. Eleazar David has friends in Bordeaux who will look after you . . ."

Marie groaned and shook her head despairingly. "It is too late for that. Girald is a born hunter. He would kill you, Robert, and I am not worth anyone's life."

"You are my life," I whispered.

"Stop it," she begged. "You are living in a romance and it blinds you to the nightmare."

"I know what I am doing," I lied. "All I need to know is how we can get out of the castle tonight."

"There is no way out. They lower the iron grilles in the gatehouses at dusk. There are two other doors through the curtain wall, one beneath the hall where the men-at-arms sleep and one behind the kitchens which they use for throwing out rubbish, but both will be locked."

"Then I will steal the keys from one of the guardrooms," I said. "Meet me at midnight by the door behind the kitchens. Promise me you will."

Marie stared into my eyes. "I will promise if you will promise me . . ."

Just then we heard footsteps, and Girald walked into the chapel. Marie let go of my hands and crossed herself, then turned and hurried out, avoiding Girald's eyes as she passed him. He smiled and strolled towards me.

"What is my wife's confession?" he asked.

"That is between me and God," I protested.

"I am between you and God," said Girald darkly, "and have a right to know what my wife says in my own castle."

He did not seem to be joking. I knew it was sacrilege to betray a confession, but as Marie had not made any I decided the only thing I ran the risk of betraying was myself.

"Very well, then," I said. "She asked God's forgiveness for hating her husband."

Girald laughed heartily. "Good. I like to know where I stand."

"She told me you are spending her dowry on the walls of your castle."

"True," said Girald, "but that is for her own protection."

"She would not need protecting if you and your men-at-arms were at Berwick helping the King," I said hotly. "You would not need to heighten your walls against the Scots if you had the courage to face them in battle."

Girald answered me with a derisive slow handclap. "Poor little monk," he said, "you peer round the pillars of your cloister and think only you can tell good from evil. It will be an evil day for me if the King sets the Three Lions flying over Berwick. That would make him strong, good for no one and evil for me, because if ever he is strong he will want revenge on Earl Thomas and then he will want it on me. The Scots will never come here – they prefer farms, and villages, and abbeys – but Edward might, and that is why I'm building a fortress strong enough to keep out a king."

"Then why," I asked, "is Earl Thomas fighting at Berwick."

"Because the best way to make the siege fail is by being

there," said Girald gaily. "And when it fails, the bishops and barons who have gathered round Edward will fail with it, and Earl Thomas will once more be the power in this realm. So will I, and when that bright day dawns I will need a castle fine enough for a man of my influence. One way or another my wife's dowry will be well spent."

The shadows were deepening in the corners of the chapel. It was almost the hour of Vespers.

"My lord," I said, "it is late for me to set out on my journey back. Might I beg a night's hospitality?"

"Only if you will not mind sleeping in the stables with the workmen," said Girald.

"Our Saviour was born in a stable," I replied, with a face glowing with devotion. "I will pray that in the morning you will have changed your mind and decided to help the Abbey of Fountains."

Girald guffawed and turned to leave. "Pray all you want; and if you stop to think where Fortune can be found, perhaps in the morning you'll come running to me and beg to be my chaplain."

Supper in the hall was an ordeal. The blazing log fire breathed new life into the smells of the unwashed men-at-arms and the slopsoaked rushes on the floor. At the high table the frail Lady de Ros dabbed at her offended nostrils with a muskball. Whenever I stole a glance at Marie she had her eyes on her dish as she patiently endured Girald's sarcastic gallantries.

"Are you any good with dice?" asked the archer.

I shook my head. "Is that how you pass your evenings?"

"There's not much choice round here," he said. "It's either wine and a girl or wine and a game of dice, unless you're on the guard. All you get then is the game of dice."

The meal did not end like the suppers I remembered in Richmond Castle, where the highest ladies and the lowest scullions sat and listened to the troubadours. As soon as the tables were cleared of food, the lords de Ros shepherded their ladies away to the privacy of the west tower, leaving the men-at-arms to drink until the wine ran out and the serving girls ran for their lives. Soon it was not proper for a monk to be there at all, and I took the excuse and slipped out into the night.

I made my way to the kitchens, and lurched in with what I hoped resembled a drunken stagger.

"Wine," I commanded, "and a long spoon. There is a trick I wish to perform to the gentlemen-at-arms in the hall."

The cook scowled, wiped her hands on her apron and filled a jug with wine. "Bring me back my spoon," she ordered.

In the shadows behind the kitchens I squatted down and opened my belt-pouch, pulling out the bag of crushed henbane and black poppy and emptying it into the jug. I stirred away like an alchemist until there were no grains left floating on the surface, then I darted back into the kitchen to hand the cook her spoon and set off across the yard to where light was shining through one of the windows of the northern gatehouse.

Stumbling and swaying, I entered the guardroom where two men were playing dice at a table.

"Ah," I cried. "They told me this was where I could find a game of dice."

"What's in that jug?" asked one of the guards.

"Nothing but wine."

"Well don't stand there, man," he growled. "Pull up a stool."

They filled their wooden beakers and emptied them in one long draught, then looked contentedly at each other and laughed. One of them rattled the dice while the other refilled the beakers and handed one to me.

"We only have two cups," he said, "so in each round of

dice the one who throws the lowest score can sit and watch the other two drinking. Sup up, Brother, and let's get going."

I raised the beaker halfway to my lips, then set it quickly down on the table and staggered to my feet clutching my stomach.

"Get outside if you're going to spew," they shouted, and I ran out of the guardroom with their laughter ringing in my ears. I did not stop running until I was safely in the shadows behind the chapel.

Crouching down by one of the buttresses, I waited until the hall began to empty and men strolled arguing towards the stables or the keep. No one went near the gatehouse. Then the lights were stubbed out in the hall and Ralph the steward walked across the yard and disappeared up the stairs into the keep. A door slammed, and the castle fell silent. I counted up to a hundred then set off towards the guardroom, hobbling on legs gone stiff with the cold.

The guards had fallen from their stools and were sprawled on the floor, their mouths open and their faces drained of colour, the slow rise and fall of their chests the only sign of life. Hanging from a spike on the wall was a ring of nine keys, and grabbing it I hurried out along the wall to the small doorway behind the kitchens. The seventh key turned the lock, and when I lifted the latch the door swung open and I found myself staring across the inner moat to the stakes of the palisade and the dark trees beyond.

Sighing with relief I closed the door and settled down beside it to wait. I was half asleep when a dark shape flickered against the night, a hand shook me gently by the shoulder and I looked up to see Marie dressed in a brown hooded cloak and soft leather riding buskins, her face as white as the moon. She put a finger to her lips and pointed at the door; I sprang up and opened it and we stepped out of the castle.

Beneath our feet a trail of rubbish led down into the fetid slough of the moat. We turned and followed the nettle-grown bank beneath the walls until we were stopped by the round tower of the gatehouse. It jutted out into the moat, leaving only the narrowest of ledges at the foot of its smooth face. I groped my way round with my cheek pressed against the stone, ducking needlessly as I passed under the glowing lancet of the silent guardroom; Marie shuffled round on her heels with her back to the tower and her eyes closed. We pushed and pulled each other up into the arch of the gateway, took a last look through the iron grille at the sleeping castle, and a few moments later we were over the drawbridge, through the outer gateway, across the outer moat and into the meadow beyond.

As soon as we were safe among the trees Marie reached into the folds of her cloak, drew out two dark lumps the size of prayer-books and offered me one.

"Gingerbread," she told me, "the only thing I shall miss about Helmsley Castle."

At the break of dawn we heard the bells of Prime ringing out from Rievaulx, and in the first rays of sunlight we came out of the forest into the fields that lined the valley floor beneath the white abbey.

We had taken some ten steps down the open lane when a hunting horn blew high above us, and turning we saw three horsemen on the rim of the valley. Then they yelled and urged their horses down towards us through the trees.

"The abbey," I hissed, and we ran for our lives.

The hunting horn blew again – the riders were out of the trees and onto the valley floor. We were running with the Devil at our back, flailing at the earth with our feet and sobbing for breath as the abbey seemed never to come nearer. A brown-robed lay brother appeared in one of the doorways and began running towards us. We could see his lips move as he shouted to us, but all we could hear were the hoofbeats drumming closer down the lane and all I could think of was the way the Templar had writhed in the saddle when the arrow struck him in the back.

A manacle of fire snapped round one of my ankles and threw me sideways into a blackthorn hedge. I sprawled to the ground while the hoofbeats thundered past me, and rolled over to see Girald turning his horse, coiling in a whip and drawing back his arm for a second strike. As I stumbled to my feet Marie ran past me and clawed at his stirrup.

"No," she wailed. "Not him. I made him do it."

Girald grabbed her by the hair and smiled at me, then swung back his arm and let fly with the whip. Pain burned into my head and I was lifted off my feet and flung into darkness.

Chapter Nine

THE PENANCE

I WOKE UP screaming at the pain in my eyes. I tried to tear them out but they were tightly bandaged with damp cloth that smelt of rosewater. In answer to my cries, I heard sandals flapping across a stone floor; a bony hand gripped the back of my neck and lifted me into a sitting position and another pressed a wooden bowl to my lips.

"Drink this," said a gentle voice.

I swallowed a mouthful of briny liquid which left grains on my tongue – crushed seeds of poppy and henbane.

"Where is Marie?" I asked.

The gentle voice wavered with embarrassment. "Lady de Ros has returned to Helmsley with her husband."

The bowl was pressed to my lips again and I sucked at it greedily. I wished I could sleep for a thousand years.

The next morning I lay in darkness listening to the bells ringing the hours and the regulated footsteps of the abbey day. I was drugged to ease the pain, but my mind drifted through sharp dreams of the joy of Marie's touch and the despair of the race towards the abbey, of Girald spitting over the rampart and Eleazar saying, "It is time you learnt to accept powerlessness."

Some time after dinner I heard footsteps, and someone sat down on the edge of my bed.

"Robert, I am Abbot Oswald. Are you well enough to talk?"

"Yes, Father."

"Good. Tell me, are you truly from the Abbey of Fountains?"

"Yes, Father. That much is true."

"Are you ready to make your confession?"

I was readier than I knew. The words came tumbling out, the whole story from the day I first hid the truth from Brother Ambrose, the day I first met Marie. Three months had given me more memories than the rest of my life put together, and the longer I talked the angrier I grew that it had to be spoken of as something wrong.

"You are very proud of yourself," said Abbot Oswald. "Can you not see what you have done? You have succumbed to one temptation after another, brought dishonour on this poor woman and shame on our Order."

"It was not temptation," I protested. "It was love."

"You were possessed by this woman," he said. "Possessed and consumed. To you it was the newest feeling in the world. It is like that, once, for all young men, and it is your long youth in a sheltered cloister which made it so unbearably intense for you. These things pass, and how different they look when a few years have gone by."

"How do I live knowing she is at Girald's mercy?" I asked.

The Abbot sighed. "We will pray for her." He laid his hand on mine. "And we will pray for you to recover your strength and your stillness."

In the evening they took off my bandages, but my eyelids were too swollen to open. I saw the dawn as if through a window streaked with rain, as a shimmering of light and colours, and in the course of the morning my sight grew clear again. In the afternoon they took me out into the small infirmary yard, wrapped me in a blanket and left me propped against one of the pillars of the cloister. The wind was blowing leaves off the trees above the abbey, and I watched them come swirling down to land at my feet, curling at the tips like holly but the colour of blood and rust.

Two mornings later, I was summoned to the chapter house to kneel in penitence before the Abbot's chair while the assembled brotherhood watched me curiously from their benches along the walls.

"Brother Robert," said Abbot Oswald, "it is not for us to pass judgement on what you have done, but we reproach you for the lies you told us when you first asked our hospitality, and for those we will set you a penance. I do not want you to see it as a punishment, but as a vigil to clear your mind of all that has passed and to prepare you to return to your own cloister at the Abbey of Fountains. Your penance will be to perform the task we believed you were undertaking. You will complete your pilgrimage to Whitby, and pray for yourself and your brothers at the Shrine of St. Hilda."

The monks were smiling, signalling their warmth and goodwill, but it was wasted on me.

"What if I cannot clear my mind?" I asked.

"I never said it would be easy," said Abbot Oswald. "Your true penance will be to live with what you have done."

The road led east, and I set out with an escort in the shape of Brother John, the abbey treasurer. He kept the vow of silence until we were out of sight of Rievaulx, but after that he talked and talked and there was no stopping him. He plied me with questions about Fountains and the wealth of her granges, then went on to tell me all he knew about the wool trade, which seemed to have been his one and only passion since before I was born.

We crossed three river valleys and came in the evening to Lastingham, a village set in a green dale between rolling moors, on one of which was a grange belonging to St. Mary's Abbey. We went there for food and shelter.

"How did you come by that evil wound?" asked the black-robed monk who welcomed us into the grange hall.

"He fought in the white battle," said Brother John quickly, "and has undertaken a pilgrimage to Whitby to pray for another of our brothers who was gravely wounded."

It appeared that while the truth could never be hidden from God, it had at all costs to be hidden from old rivals like the black monks in case they repeated it with embellishments all the way to the Pope in Avignon.

"If you are a pilgrim," said the Benedictine, "you must not leave without praying at the Shrine of St. Cedd. It was built by the Blessed Stephen."

"Yes, Robert must see it," agreed Brother John. "I will take him there straight after supper."

The Shrine was a great crypt, hundreds of years old, built with thick round pillars and an arched roof of huge blocks, and so cold that my breath steamed in the candlelight. The icy stone froze our knees as we recited the prayers of Compline.

As we left, Brother John ignored the offerings casket. "I can't bring myself to part with a groat for the Blessed Stephen," he whispered. "His vanity is the only altar in that crypt."

"Who was he?" I asked.

"You don't know?" asked Brother John with some surprise. "He was a monk who wanted to be Abbot of Whitby, who was so disgruntled when he failed that he ran off with some of his brothers to found an abbey of his own. One look at Lastingham was enough to convince him that St. Cedd was good for a few pilgrims, so he settled down and started building, and with an eye on his income he began with the crypt. He sent his brothers all over the North to beg donations for the rekindling of an ancient centre of light."

"What went wrong?" I asked looking at the worthy but simple stone church that stood over the crypt.

"Surely you know?" said Brother John. "Stephen found that only the poor were concerned about St. Cedd, so he decided to move on and found an abbey closer to the lords and riches of the land. That is how he came to York and founded the Abbey of St. Mary's."

I was struck by the pattern it made. "And it was from St. Mary's that brothers later ran away to found the Abbey of Fountains?"

"Yes indeed," said Brother John. "So in journeying to Whitby you are travelling back to the farthest root of your abbey. That is why we believed your story when you first came to Rievaulx."

The next day we both travelled with an escort, in the shape of two bondsmen of the lord of Egton who were taking a train of mules over the moors. The road led over a broad high plateau of heather waste, pagan stones, and stunted rowan trees, and the long miles gave Brother John ample time to explain to me how the lime in the panniers of the mules was used to mellow the bitter soil of the northern valleys.

Late that afternoon we came down into Rosedale, where farms, ironstone workings, and an abbey all clustered on the valley floor, a green ribbon of life in the bleak heart of the moors.

"Please do not be offended," said Brother John, "but I think it might be best, when we reach the abbey, if you go straight to the guest-house and leave the greetings to me."

"More black monks?" I asked.

"No, white nuns," he replied. "Good sisters, examples to us all, but not one of them has a head for figures. I have been sent to help them draw up their Martinmas accounts."

So when we reached the abbey I let Brother John point me towards the guest-house, then I walked quickly to the door, my hood pulled forward over my face to prevent any novice from catching sight of me and being possessed by the Devil. In the morning I was hurried out onto the road with the bondsmen, and Brother John waved goodbye with much relief. I still remember the clear and magical singing that was coming from the church as I left.

The road continued over higher moors, along wide ridgeways marked with tall stone crosses. A bitter wind was blowing, and my eyes streamed with tears each time a new squall blew into our faces. The bondsmen took pity on me and stretched me across the panniers of the sturdiest mule, and I was carried down into Eskdale like a sackful of relics, to spend the night sprawled on a blanket in the smelly warmth of the Lord of Egton's manor hall.

At daybreak I set off alone down the valley, to follow the river to the sea. A wooded gorge gave way to hamlets and granges, then I heard seagulls shrieking in the sky and caught my first glimpse of Whitby Abbey, towering on its clifftop above the sea in brown stone pinnacles that cut into the sky.

Huddled beside the harbour at the foot of the cliff was a village where folk with faces leathery from hard weather haggled in Nordic voices and the gulls sat on the rooftops waiting for the fishing boats. I was passing a bakery when a boy my age came out carrying a basket of loaves. He was wearing the black cassock of a Benedictine novice and he stared at my scar.

"God's blessing on you," I greeted him. "Can you lead me to the Shrine of St. Hilda?"

"Willingly," he said. "What happened to your head?"

I shut him up with the story of the white battle. We climbed a steep pathway that wound up the cliff, and reached the abbey as the monks were coming out of Vespers.

"Is the Shrine in the church?" I asked.

"First you must eat with us," insisted the boy, so I gave

into the smell of the loaves and let him lead me along the cloister to the refectory.

The monks of Whitby made no pretence at a vow of silence, and the chatter as they ate was fit to rival the hall at Helmsley. The novice was called Brother Fabian, and he plied me with helping after helping of baked herrings and kept my cup brimming with wine that came from Aquitaine. All around me I saw silver dishes, and the Abbot sat like a baron with a falcon on his wrist. After the fish came a choice between gooseberry pie and apple and cinnamon wafers.

"You must be rich to live so well," I murmured.

"We have not half the wealth of Fountains or Rievaulx," said Brother Fabian with a laugh. "Which is worse, a greed for the good life or a greed for wool?"

I could find no answer to that.

"I meant it as a jest," he said quickly. "You are most welcome. The prior tells me you are the first pilgrim we have had in five years, since before the famine and the Scots started crossing the Tees. Let us hope you are the first of many now that the truce has been signed."

"What truce?" I asked.

"We only heard yesterday," said Brother Fabian. "King Edward and Robert Bruce have pledged that neither will take up arms against the other for the space of two years."

"Thank God," I said, then checked myself. "What happened at Berwick?" I asked.

"The siege fell apart," said Brother Fabian with a shrug.

"How?" I asked suspiciously.

"I gather it was for the news of Archbishop William's battle. Earl Thomas and the northern barons came haring home to protect their lands. The King could not take Berwick without them, and with winter drawing on he was forced to make the truce to give himself a safe journey south; so something good came out of something bad."

As I stared into my wine, I heard two voices in my

memory. The first was Archbishop William's, promising a victory to heal the realm. The second was Girald's, promising that if Edward failed at Berwick then Thomas would be stronger than ever. Girald had been right; the Wheel of Fortune had spun again, throwing Edward down and bringing Thomas back to power. Nothing would stop him now.

When the meal was over I made my way into the candlelit church. The Shrine was the ugliest I had ever seen, a barbaric boulder of marble plated with gold and studded with jewels. It told me so little about St. Hilda that I did not even try to pray there.

I walked out of the abbey onto the clifftop to stare out to sea. The clouds were sailing fast across the sky, and when the moon shone between them it shivered a reflection on the crest of the waves. The wind cut through my cassock like a knife; it howled around my ears like a hundred ghosts, and I was drunk enough to wonder if my father were among them.

"Did you see all this coming?" I asked him. "Were you trying to tell me that knights don't live for chivalry any more? Is that why you shut me up in an abbey?" I belched loudly. "Well, now I know, and now what do you want me to do?"

The wind gave no answer.

"Damn it," I shouted. "The only difference between our hells is that mine is a silent one."

I dropped to my knees and felt the ring knock against my chest, then I wept like a baby, staring out to sea and chilled to the bone.

When I turned back towards the glowing windows of the abbey, I suddenly remembered the story of St. Hilda . . . She had been one of the first Christians in the North, the niece of a powerful king, and long after he was dead and the land torn apart by war she had come to Whitby to live a life of prayer; to burn herself as incense as she prayed for a world made whole. There were so few abbeys in those days that she could have had any of the gentle valleys of the North, but she had chosen a clifftop at the ends of the earth.

There it was, the quest that was older than the silver dishes and the worries over the price of wool, the sacrifice that could still be made if only one had the love to make it.

Four days later I reached York.

Brother Ambrose was sitting by the fire. He gave a gasp, sprang to his feet and rushed over to fold me in his arms.

"Robert, Robert," he almost sobbed. "I've been praying you would come back." He reached up to touch my face. "What in God's name has happened to you? Where have you been? What was all that pig-swill about a sister in Richmond?"

I told him the whole story from beginning to end, and he was so staggered he forgot to pout. "Forgive me," I said at the end. "I never wanted to betray you."

"Then don't talk nonsense," he said. "You followed your heart, and that can never be called a betrayal. Dear me, though. Abbot Walter will have my skin for this. I should never have let a young novice out of my sight."

"Forgive me," I said again.

"Oh, we'll survive," he said cheerfully. "All that matters is that you're safe. I've been terrified by the thought that I'd have to go back without you."

"When do we leave?"

"Tomorrow," said Brother Ambrose. He gave a pout of thoughtful consideration. "Which means we have a special task ahead of us. Mistress Matilda made a miracle of a pie this afternoon, and it would be a sin for it to go uneaten."

Chapter Ten

THE PARLIAMENT OF HATE

So I returned to the Abbey of Fountains, convinced it would be my home for the rest of my life.

Abbot Walter set me the same penance I had been set five years before: the abbey accounts. Nothing could have been more deadening. Two of our best lowland granges had been stripped bare by the Scots on their way home from the white battle. The upland granges were still reeling from the famine, and we could find neither the lay brothers to farm them nor the money to restock their herds. The longer they decayed the less they produced, and the less they produced the more unlikely it became that we would ever have the money to repair the damage. As the days shortened into winter, Brother Ambrose and I were left buried alive in the muniment room, our eyes stung by candlesmoke and our minds bent double as we calculated the harvests we would need to save the abbey from a plunge into debt.

Curiously enough, Earl Thomas made no move to take away our granges of Wiggesham and Norton. It was curious because he now had the power to do whatever he wanted. He refused to attend the January parliament in York, letting it be known that he no longer trusted the King or his ministers, and the result was a stagnation of all governance in which the realm was left to drift. Edward's answer was to sail away to France and the delights of Paris, leaving Thomas the unnamed king of the North, enthroned in Pontefract Castle, dismissing any sheriffs and judges who were not to his liking and replacing them with men of his own. It was exactly as Girald had predicted.

Then it rained all summer, and the harvest failed. The misery of famine began all over again.

For the abbey accounts, it was a turn of the screw. The wool clip was so poor we had to borrow to make up our revenues, and no sooner had we signed away any wool profits for three years to come than the winter came on so wet that our remaining flocks were decimated by liver rot. Brother Ambrose took the only course of action that was left, and drew up a plan to be read out in the chapter house. So it was that Abbot Walter ordered that our six highest Pennine granges be abandoned, the lands opened up by our forbears be left to revert to the wild and our flocks brought down to the lowlands where at least we had the lay brothers to tend them. One of the older monks cried. From where I sat, over accounts that still showed no sign of improvement, it looked as if the Wheel of Fortune were spinning against us.

The second and last spring of the Scottish truce came round, and with it the second anniversary of the day I met Marie. She was ever in my mind. It was always at night, when I lay in the silence and darkness with the ring heavy on my chest, that memories returned like an enchantment whose magic grew stronger with time. In my dreams I felt her touch and heard her voice, and I came alive, but always I woke up to join the procession of coughing old men who shuffled their way down into the church.

Then, one afternoon when the sun had made a rare appearance and we were working with the windows open, a brother knocked on the door of the muniment room to tell Brother Ambrose and me that Abbot Walter wished to see us. We found him sitting in the cloister, holding a parchment which he waved at us as we arrived.

"We have been summoned," he said; "summoned to

attend our Lord of Lancaster at his manor of Sherburn-in-Elmet on St. Paul's Eve."

"So he has remembered the granges," said Brother Ambrose wearily.

"So it would seem," agreed the Abbot.

"What will we do?" I asked.

Abbot Walter gave a wry smile. "Give them to him. The most we can hope for is that it all happens graciously. I want you to write out a deed of gift, and I will take you with me in case I have need of a scribe."

"Hmm. Is Robert the wisest choice as your companion?" asked Brother Ambrose, seeing the look of dismay on my face and doing his best to save me.

"Indeed he is," said the Abbot. "He will know better than to run around getting himself into trouble."

It was only a ride of two days from the abbey to Sherburn-in-Elmet, but it was not a happy journey.

Everywhere we looked we saw the scars of famine. There was so little seedcorn that we passed field after field that had not even been given a spring ploughing because there was nothing to sow it with. Other fields which should have been swathes of midsummer growth were nothing but a few clumps of rain-rotted barley. There was hardly one healthy farm animal in all the Vale of York, and in the villages we passed through, the women held up their screaming children and begged for alms.

By the middle of the second afternoon we had run out of small coins and were forced to run the gauntlet of a village where we had nothing to give. The women screamed abuse at us and the boys pelted the flanks of our horses with clods of mud.

To our relief we were soon on a larger road along which were riding a party of men-at-arms and churchmen. At their centre, under the banner of St. Peter, was Archbishop

William of York. He greeted us warmly and invited us to ride with him.

"I am grateful for the chance to ask your Grace's counsel," said Abbot Walter. "We have been summoned to attend the Earl of Lancaster . . ."

"How strange," said the Archbishop. "So have I."

The further we travelled the more riders we came across. There were knights with their retinues, and towards sunset we met the Bishop of Carlisle. It began to look as though every magnate in the North had been summoned to Sherburn-in-Elmet.

The following morning, in the tapestried splendour of Earl Thomas's manor hall, the mystery only deepened.

The hall was crowded, and Abbot Walter and I found ourselves crushed at the back of a gathering of prelates headed by Archbishop William and the Bishops of Durham and Carlisle. Every other inch of space was taken up by more barons and knights than I could count. Whispers went round that several of the most powerful lords of the Welsh Marches were present, and all of them, like us, were quietly sweating in the moist heat of the June day and waiting for Earl Thomas.

When he came he made his entrance like a king, preceded by a knight who wore his livery and who carried his sword. He took his seat on the dais, let his gaze sweep regally over the assembly, then nodded to the knight, who stepped forward and assumed the role of his master's mouthpiece.

"My lords and prelates," he said sonorously; "pray receive the welcome of my Lord Thomas, Earl of Lancaster, Lincoln, and Derby, and his thanks for your attendance. He has summoned you here to ask for your counsel on how to combat the grave evils that beset this realm; namely the bad character of the King's ministers, the banishments decreed by the King without judgement of peers, the injustice of the royal taxes on wool, and the imprudent treaties that have been made with foreign kingdoms. These are matters my Lord Thomas wishes to remedy if you will only advise him on what remedies to pursue."

The speech was greeted with general bewilderment by the churchmen around me, but the barons seemed to find it highly pleasing. Earl Thomas beckoned to the knight, spoke softly into his ear, and the knight then spoke again.

"As the hall is so crowded, the prelates may care to remove themselves to the house of the rector, on the far side of the court. There they will be able to deliberate unhindered."

Archbishop William led us out into the fresh air. No sooner were we gathered in the rector's house than the Bishop of Durham burst into a torrent of denunciation.

"This whole assembly is an outrage," he said hotly. "Can you not see what Thomas is doing? He is asking us to perform an obscene parody of a parliament, with that knight playing the part of the chancellor and with Thomas as king. Who in God's name does he think he is?"

"Calm yourself, Louis," said Archbishop William. "Thomas thinks he is a power unto himself, and the fact that we are here would seem to prove that he is. What alarms me is the number of barons he suddenly has at his beck and call, and the delight he took in displaying them to us."

"All part of the game," replied the Bishop, his fleshy cheeks quivering. "For years now he has been pretending to be King of England. We cannot allow him to do it to us. We must leave at once."

"If I might speak?" asked the Bishop of Carlisle, and all eyes turned to him. "We must also remember the things we pretend to ourselves," he said quietly. "I was struck by the reference to imprudent treaties with foreign kingdoms. The truce with the Scots will be over in a few months, and as we approach that day of uncertainty, are we going to pretend to ourselves that King Edward will be here to protect us? The men we will need with us are the barons who at this moment in time are standing beside Earl Thomas. We must resist them, but we cannot afford to offend them."

There was an uneasy silence, then Archbishop William tugged at his beard and spoke musingly.

"We could always reply to Earl Thomas that we will gladly help him to protect the land from the Scots, but that we humbly beg that discussion of all other matters be deferred until the next parliament of the realm."

Everyone murmured their relieved assent.

"Good," said the Archbishop. "Have we a scribe among us?"

Abbot Walter pushed me forward, and that is how I came to write the reply of the prelates of the North to the summons of the Earl of Lancaster. Archbishop William read the finished parchment and handed it back to me.

"Excellent. Be so kind as to take it to Earl Thomas, and keep your eyes open. Read the signs on his face as he reads it."

Clutching the scroll, I crossed the courtyard and elbowed my way into the hall. Many of the barons were clustered round the dais and looking pleased; others were standing back with a more detached air. I had to wait a while before the chance came to present Earl Thomas with the parchment. As he read it his mouth curled into a smile, and when he had finished he spoke to me in the voice of a man who is content.

"Thank the prelates for their counsel and inform them I have no further need of their attendance. They are welcome to stay and dine, but are free to leave."

His wave of dismissal was so regal that, without thinking, I bowed. Some barons nearby burst out laughing, and I was blushing as I ducked between them and made for the door. I had not gone ten steps across the courtyard when a voice called out behind me.

"Brother Scarface."

I should have run, but instead I turned round. Girald de Ros was strolling towards me.

"I'm glad we have the chance to talk," he said cheerfully. "I want to know why you ran off with the little slut. I've given up trying to get the truth out of her."

He smiled as I winced, and he was not the only one with two years' worth of festering hate inside him.

"Perhaps they'll tell you in hell," I said, "but I will never talk about her to dung like you."

He hit me so hard that I sprawled on my back in the mud; then he drew his sword. The men-at-arms who were lazing against the walls of the courtyard stopped their dice-games to watch, but no one moved so much as a toenail to come to my help.

"Go on," I begged Girald. "It makes no difference to me. You took away my life two years ago."

"How refreshing to see a knight performing deeds of valour," cut in a voice I dimly recognised. It belonged to a knight who was striding towards us from the doorway of the hall, and one look at his sandy hair and grey eyes wrenched me back seven years to the very day I first met Girald de Ros. It was Sir Andrew Harclay.

"Stay out of this, Harclay," ordered Girald. "I have a just quarrel with this wart of a monk."

"I am here to relish it, not to stop it," replied Harclay mockingly. "I seem to remember that when I made my oath of knighthood, I swore to protect the church. Perhaps you have forgotten yours, or are you just going out of your way to give me a perfect reason to kill you?"

Girald glared with exasperation, but Harclay simply stood there, one hand resting lightly on his scabbard and the other hooked into his belt. The threat seemed to gather strength the longer the silence lasted. Finally Girald scowled, slammed his sword back into its scabbard, and forced a laugh.

"Time will tell," he said, "which of us will live to spit on the other's grave."

"I'm looking forward to it," replied Harclay, keeping perfectly still. Girald gave him a last withering look, then turned on his heel and stormed off into the hall. Only then did Harclay walk over and help me to my feet.

"How do monks make such mean enemies?" he asked with a smile.

"Don't you remember me?" I asked.

He peered into my face a moment, then uttered a mild oath. "Robert de Falaise." Then he threw back his head and roared with laughter.

"What is so funny?" I asked.

"Only that Stephen dumped you in an abbey for the very purpose of saving you from moments like the one you have just lived. It seems there is no dodging fate." He jerked his thumb towards the hall. "What was on the parchment you gave to Earl Thomas?"

I told him the reply of the prelates.

"Neatly put," he said. "There is still a little wisdom in this blighted land. Come on."

He began to walk me towards the rector's house. "Are you with Earl Thomas now?" I asked hesitantly.

"God forbid," said Harclay. "I hold Carlisle for the King, but when Thomas summoned me I had to come and see what he wanted. After all these years I am still only a landless knight, which means I have to take great care always to know which way the wind is blowing. That is another of the troubles your father wanted to spare you."

"So you follow the Wheel of Fortune?" I asked.

Harclay gave me a sideways glance. "Even if you never intend to ride it, you still need to know which way it is spinning."

By this time we were entering the house of the rector. The prelates listened intently while I told them of the Earl's dismissal, and when I had finished the Archbishop turned to Harclay.

"Sir Andrew, can you tell us the meaning of all this?"

"The bad character of the King's ministers, for want of a better phrase," said Harclay. "Hugh Despenser has been trying to carve himself a kingdom in Wales, and Edward has broken half the laws on the statutes to help him get what he wants. Men have been banished to get them off their lands, and that is what has brought the lords of the Welsh March running to Thomas. He summoned you here to impress them, and it worked. Some sixty magnates have just sworn never to rest until Despenser has been destroyed."

"Lord deliver us," said the Bishop of Durham. "It's the story of Piers Gaveston all over again."

"With a difference, your Grace," said Harclay. "Edward has never forgiven the barons for what they did to Gaveston, and weak as he is, he will never let the pattern repeat itself. That is a great pity, because Gaveston was merely a fool, but Despenser is clever and hated with good reason, and if the King goes on protecting him I can name you many good men who will stand with Earl Thomas if it turns into a tournament."

"And you, Sir Andrew?" asked the Archbishop. "Where will you stand?"

Harclay laughed grimly. "In the castle of Carlisle, answering any summons I receive by pleading the need for someone to remain on the border."

Archbishop William nodded and rose to his feet. "Well, since the Earl has no further need of us, I suggest we leave at once."

Abbot Walter and I were mounting our horses in the midday glare when Harclay walked over and squinted at me.

"You are an ungrateful brat, Robert. You could at least thank me for saving your life."

"Saving your life?" repeated Abbot Walter wonderingly.

"A jest, Father," said Harclay. He winked at me. "You may be able to save mine one day."

"I doubt it," I said sadly, "but if ever you need a scribe . . ."

The next parliament of the realm was held three weeks later at Westminster. By the end of July it was the talk of the North.

Earl Thomas had gone to London with half the magnates of England at his back, all of them decked out in green and white coat armour paid for by the Earl and giving them the appearance of some weird new order of knighthood. For days Edward refused even to hear their petitions, then he gave in and the wrangling began, and at the end of a week he gave in again and agreed that Despenser should be banished. Earl Thomas rode home claiming that he had saved England.

"More fool Thomas," said Brother Ambrose. "Three times they banished Gaveston, and three times he returned. Hugh Despenser will be back just as soon as he runs out of money."

We had other things to worry about. The harvest was pitiful and the famine was biting deeper.

Then in early November, not long after Martinmas, Abbot Walter received a summons to attend Earl Thomas in Doncaster. This time he left me behind and rode with the cellarer and two lay brothers. He returned a week later looking ten years older, and gathered us all at once into the chapter house.

"The Earl wishes it to be known," he said, "that King Edward has been helping Hugh Despenser to live a life of piracy on the south coast, a crime so grievous that unless the King repents at once, the magnates will be forced to defend their rights by show of arms."

He paused, and the challenge of open rebellion echoed in the silence.

"And will the King repent?" asked Brother Ambrose.

"That is what I asked Archbishop William on our ride home," said the Abbot. "He told me that the Earls of Pembroke and Arundel are raising an army for the King. The royal castles are being garrisoned." His eyes swept round our faces in a long tired glance. "So we must pray for the deliverance of England."

Chapter Eleven

THE LESSON OF THE BORDER

ONCE THE WINTER had set in, the roads became a quagmire and for months we had no news of the world. England might be burning, but we spent our days in the separate reality of prayer, and the monotony of the Rule mixed with a famine diet reduced us all to the strange walking sleep they call the melancholy of the cloister.

One afternoon in March I left the manuscript I was copying to gather dust and went off to sit by the abbey fishpond. The valley was filled with smoky drizzle, and there were frail snowdrops and stubby primroses in the wet grass. I heard a sound of horses' bridles and the clatter of hooves in the distance by the abbey gate and smiled at the thought of all my brothers swooping on the visitors like ducks on a crumb. At least there would be something new to whisper about for the next three weeks.

Then I heard Brother Ambrose calling my name. Standing up, I could just see him peering into the trees from the footbridge over the stream. He beckoned to me furiously.

"Robert, you are wanted in the Abbot's house. Hurry."

Standing by the Abbot's fireplace with rain dripping off his chain-mail was Sir Andrew Harclay.

Abbot Walter showed me a parchment. "Sir Andrew has a writ with the King's seal demanding that he be given any assistance he requires. He is asking me to allow you to enter his service."

"I need a scribe, Robert," said Harclay. "Someone to write the chronicle of what is about to happen."

"What is that?" I asked.

"I will tell you as we ride. There is very little time."

"Wait just a moment," pleaded Abbot Walter. "You are the first visitor we have had for months. You cannot go before you have told us what is happening in the world."

"I wish I had the time, Father," said Harclay. "Robert will tell you everything when he returns." He frowned and paused. "You have not heard then, about the Cathedral of Ely?"

"What of it?" asked the Abbot.

"The central tower has fallen down. Much of the building is ruined, and all England is debating what it means."

The Abbot's face brightened and he glowed with Bernardine zeal. "It can only mean that at long last the bishops are being punished for their vanities."

I knelt to receive his blessing.

At the hour of Compline we rode into Ripon. The sky was dark above the towers of St. Wilfrid's Minster but the town was ablaze with torchlight. The market-place was crowded with soldiers; border veterans with faces like boiled leather and pikes and longbows. Harclay dismounted and handed the reins of his horse to a sergeant-at-arms.

"You'll find a soup kitchen in the merchants' hall," he told me. "Go and see if you can bring yourself to swallow any of the swill they're doling out."

I limped off, rubbing my rump, and queued for the reward of a slab of greyish bread and a bowl of kale broth. Thus fortified I wandered around the market-place trying to see it all with the eye of a chronicler: the soldiers cleaning their weapons, the gossiping frightened townsfolk, the excited laughter of the girls who gathered on the street corners in twos and threes. From time to time I caught sight of

Harclay, talking to his captains and gesturing with his hands as though he were giving them precise instructions of the utmost importance.

It was well after sunset when he strode back to his horse and ordered his trumpeter to sound the advance. The army wound slowly down the sloping streets below the Minster, a cavalcade of mounted knights followed by troop after troop of marching footmen. We were heading east.

Once out of Ripon, the march became a slow rhythmic procession along the dark road. Harclay cantered up and down the length of the column, and at the end of one such inspection he reined back his horse to trot gently beside mine.

"So," he said, "what do you think of my army, so lovingly gathered together with the power of the King's writ?"

"It is certainly a fearful one," I replied. "Where did you find them all?"

"They are the levies of Cumberland and Westmorland, some Welsh archers, and men from every English garrison on the border."

"What about the Scots?" I asked querulously.

"Aye," said Harclay, "I'm taking a chance, but I've been expecting a raid since November and the border has been as quiet as a crypt. Then last month I discovered that Clifford and Mowbray, two of Thomas's cronies, had been slithering across it at dead of night to go and see Bruce. There are one or two people at the Scottish court who owe me favours, and I found out from them that Thomas and Bruce have signed a pact of allegiance."

"Against the King? But that is evil."

"Not evil, just stupid," corrected Harclay. "Listen to this. I managed to get hold of a letter that Thomas sent Bruce at the end of last year. The words are carefully veiled, so it would only go halfway to being evidence of treason, but do you know how he signed himself?"

"How?"

Harclay sighed. "He signed himself 'King Arthur'. Now we know the size of the poor fool's delusions."

"Forgive me for saying so, but the barons he had with him at Sherburn did not look like a delusion."

"They are now," said Harclay, and I saw that he was smiling through the darkness. "You miss such a lot by being shut away in a cloister. At New Year the King took his army straight into Wales, so fast that he caught the Lords of the March sitting in their castles where they surrendered without a fight. Mowbray, Clifford and the Earl of Hereford escaped to join Thomas, but the grand alliance had been cut in half at a stroke."

"The King acted with rare judgement," I said admiringly.

Harclay smiled again. "Let's just say the Earls of Pembroke and Arundel gave him excellent counsel, though it's true that the prospect of revenge for Gaveston is one of the few things that can still get Edward out of bed. Thomas could still have blocked their way north, but he dithered away February laying siege to the royal castle at Tickhill, and by the time it dawned on him that he ought to do something about cutting the bridges over the Trent, it was too late and Edward was across. Honestly, your abbot would make a better leader of a rebellion than Thomas."

"So what did he do?" I asked.

"He scuttled back to Pontefract to make his last stand, but a few days there seem to have changed his mind. Now he and Hereford and the whole lot of them are making a run for Scotland."

"And will Robert Bruce come south to meet them?"

"There's always the chance," agreed Harclay, "but my guess is that he'll sit on his own side of the border and laugh himself to tears at the sight of us killing each other."

"So where is Thomas now?" I asked.

"As you and I left Fountains, he and his forces should just have been arriving at Boroughbridge."

"Boroughbridge?" I repeated. "But that is only a few miles away."

"Quite," said Harclay, "and we are almost there. He'll have a fine surprise when he wakes up."

Soon afterwards we reached the great north road, and Harclay ordered those of us who were riding to dismount. The whole force began to advance on foot down the road to the river crossing. No one spoke. In the songs of the troubadours, knights gallop into battle with banners unfurled, but Harclay's men were a different breed, border veterans who moved like hunters, and their surefooted stealth made my flesh creep. It was such a far cry from the passionate rabble with whom I had approached Boroughbridge from the opposite direction two and a half years before.

The strange procession halted on the riverbank. The bridge was empty and unguarded, but the village on the far bank had so many campfires that it looked as though dark velvet had been embroidered with rubies. Harclay divided his forces, sending half his knights, archers, and pikemen, to a shallow ford downstream, and gathering the rest at the northern end of the bridge. Pasties and ale were passed round as the sky began to pale towards dawn.

The sunrise lit a land of desolation. Most of Boroughbridge was still the charred ruin that Black Douglas had left it. I made the mistake of looking east towards the meadows of the massacre.

"There has been too much death here already," I muttered.

To my surprise Harclay nodded, and for one brief moment the fear showed in his eyes. "River crossings make the best killing grounds," he said drily. "I have nightmares in which I am back in that God-forsaken valley near Stirling. The river there is called the Bannockburn, but then death traps always have friendly names." His eyes narrowed. "Thomas, you may remember, was not there on that day of hell." He swung round and signalled to the trumpeters. "Wake them up," he ordered.

A loud fanfare rang out across the river. Men staggered out of the tents that had been set up among the ruins, took one look at us and ran around shouting at each other. As the daylight grew we saw a crowd gathering round a tent which flew the azure and silver pennon of Earl Thomas. From the tops of other tents fluttered well over two dozen different heraldic banners.

"The Earl has a lot of knights with him," I remarked.

"Fix them in your memory," said Harclay. "I want every one of them listed in the chronicle."

He began pointing out the pennons and naming them to me one by one, until I knew at a glance the banners of Hereford, Clifford, Mowbray, and countless other lesser knights. Amongst them was the pennon of de Ros. I was staring at it when the crowd on the far bank parted and two fully-armoured knights came clanking towards the bridge. They were wearing no weapons.

"Thomas and Hereford," said Harclay with a smile. He unbuckled his sword-belt and passed it to a squire. "Come on, Robert. I want you to hear every word."

I followed him unwillingly out onto the bridge. The planking creaked and the waters of the Eure flowed swiftly beneath us. In the middle of the river, Harclay stopped and waited for the two earls to reach him.

"Sir Andrew!" exclaimed Earl Thomas with a jovial shout and a gleam of teeth. "Have you come to join us?"

"Nothing so pleasant, my lord," replied Harclay. "Four days ago at Tutbury the King proclaimed you both rebels, and I am here in his name to ask for your surrender."

"This cannot be," protested Earl Thomas. "It would

sadden me to see men of your worth skulking at the side of Edward of Caernarvon."

"Well, it saddens me to see good men skulking at yours," said Harclay.

Earl Thomas changed colour, and it was the Earl of Hereford who spoke next. "Try not to be foolish. You cannot stop us crossing if we have a mind to."

Harclay just smiled at him.

"Am I to understand you mean to fight over this?" asked Earl Thomas with raised eyebrows, as though the mere suggestion were ridiculous.

"In the name of the King I have asked you to surrender," said Harclay, choosing his words slowly and carefully. "In the name of the King, I hold the bridge against you; and if you attack me, with banners unfurled, it will be open treason."

The earls glowered at him.

"You won't live to regret this," said the Earl of Hereford. "We'll trample you into the mud."

They turned and clanked away as fast as their silvery armour would allow. As Harclay and I walked back to our side of the river I found my legs were shaking the way they shook the day I walked into Helmsley Castle. It seemed a bad omen if ever there were one.

The morning dragged on, and the watery March sun rose higher in the sky, and still the movements in the rebel camp were no more than a meaningless swarming as men bustled to and fro among the ruined buildings.

It was long after the hour of Terce when at last something happened. Horses were led out and saddled, and fully-armoured knights emerged from their tents and were helped onto their mounts. Soon there were almost a hundred of them, grouped around the fluttering pennons of Hereford and Clifford, and with a fanfare of trumpets they began to canter gently down towards the riverbank in a pageant of chivalry that took my breath away. I was so entranced by the spectacle that it was a moment before I grasped that they were about to charge the bridge.

"Holy Mary," I whispered, and my hand went to my ring.

"The poor fools," said Harclay, shaking his head. He turned to the archers. "I want them all on the bridge before a single arrow is loosed."

The knights were now thundering across the far bank, and I watched transfixed as they clattered onto the bridge. They were yelling their names like talismans, waving their swords above their heads, and the timbers of the bridge shook beneath their weight. Harclay's men moved like a well-oiled hinge. The archers slotted arrows to their bows and the pikemen blocked our end of the bridge in ranks six men deep. The noise of the charge became deafening, but Harclay just scratched his chin and waited until the whole bridge was a seething mass of horsemen and the knights of the vanguard were within a few yards of our side of the river.

"Now," he called out.

The air lisped with arrows, then men and horses shrieked and screamed and the charge lost all shape. In one great writhe of agony the knights twisted and collided and crashed through the splintering parapets to plunge into the river, where the weight of their armour dragged them straight to the bottom. In the same moment the remains of the vanguard reached our end of the bridge and impaled themselves on a wall of pikes. It was a shambles. I hid my face in my hands and waited for it to end.

When at last I looked up the bridge was empty except for the splayed figures of the dead. On the far bank the soldiers of the rebel camp were swarming protectively around the few knights who had returned. Close at hand I saw Harclay bending over the figures of two dead pikemen. They were all the attack had cost us.

Harclay walked over to me. "Well?" he asked. "Did you count all the banners?"

"I have never seen anything so brave," I said, "but the way you fought them . . ."

"Go on," he said. "Spit it out."

"It was not chivalrous."

He grimaced, then squatted down beside me and ran his hands through his hair.

"When I was a boy, Robert, I thought the most glorious thing in the world was a charging knight. I thought that victory was a matter of courage and will, and nothing else. I dreamt of the battles I would win with my valour . . . Then one day I found myself running for my life from the valley of the Bannockburn. Robert Bruce won that battle with his mind. He forced us to charge over marshy ground where we could find no speed, then he cut us to pieces with arrows and pikes and pushed us back until we were crushed against each other and helpless. It was the lesson of the border. If Thomas had been there he would have learnt it as I did; it's not my fault he's had to wait until today."

"So what will they do now?"

"Try again, with every man they have. They have no choice. Sir Simon Ward will be on his way from York with a force of levies. By tomorrow morning they'll be surrounded."

They tried again in the middle of the afternoon. The far bank echoed with trumpets and a hundred knights on horseback rode straight for the ford that lay downstream. They were led by Earl Thomas himself, and close behind him I made out the yellow surcoat of Girald de Ros. Yelling like madmen, they urged their horses through the river, straight into a withering hail of arrows. I had an evil urge to run along the bank and ask an archer to kill Girald for me, but before I could bring myself to do it the other half of the rebel army came pouring across the bridge.

This time they came on foot, Hereford and Clifford leading several hundred men-at-arms. The archers loosed volley after volley into them, but they were too many to be stopped by arrows. They surged against the wall of pikemen and the end of the bridge became a mangled crush of hand-to-hand fighting. Harclay drew his sword and waded into the thick of it, hacking away like Richard Lionheart, but he and his squires were battered by the weight of the charge and pushed back step after step. Glancing downstream I saw Earl Thomas and his knights desperately trying to break through the pikemen on our side of the ford. There was a wild despair in their courage, so heartrending to see that I almost wished they could win.

Then three things happened on the bridge: our archers began to take their toll, Harclay struck down Clifford, and the Earl of Hereford suddenly rose up in the air, skewered from below by a pikeman who had sneaked beneath the planking. The attackers broke and fled.

I ran downstream, but at the ford it was all over. Earl Thomas and his men were flailing back towards the southern bank. It was a moment before I caught sight of the yellow surcoat I was looking for. Girald had lost his horse, his helmet, and his sword, but he was unscathed. The last I saw of him, he was running like a hare towards Boroughbridge.

It was enough to at last break the discipline of Harclay's border veterans. They began whooping and cheering, and men ran off to the woods to fetch fuel for cooking-fires. A short while later I was breaking the Rule with a succulent leg of roast rabbit when Harclay tapped me on the shoulder. Earl Thomas was walking across the bridge.

He was alone, and he had exchanged his armour for an exquisite gown trimmed with sable fur. As we reached him, he greeted us with a smile of utter nonchalance, as though we had met by chance in a rose garden.

"Well done, Sir Andrew," he said gaily. "It would seem that you have won the ribbon in this tournament."

"I can imagine how that grieves your lordship," replied Harclay.

"Yes, it grieves me," he admitted, then he thrust out his hand. "Join me, Andrew. I can make you rich. Together we . . ."

"You insult me," cut in Harclay, reducing the Earl to silence. "I will grant you a truce for the night," he said, "and in the morning you will have the same choice of surrender or battle."

"Till the morning, then," said Earl Thomas quietly, and he turned and walked back towards Boroughbridge. Harclay let out a long breath.

"Strange," he said, "the heady feeling of knowing you have broken the strongest man in England."

Soon after that the sun at last went down on that day of blood.

I was woken at first light by Harclay, who was wiping his eyes and laughing.

"Robert, come and look at this."

The Eure was covered by a mist that gave it the look of a river of steam. Over in Boroughbridge the rebel camp was almost deserted. Tents flapped open and empty, and heaps of discarded gear lay scattered around cold hearths. That was not all. Beyond the village but marching towards it was a strong force of men under the banner of Sir Simon Ward, the High Sheriff of Yorkshire.

We crossed the bridge and searched the town from end to end. House after house held wounded and dispirited men who were happy to surrender. We passed an empty tent above which fluttered the pennon of de Ros, and I knew then that we would not catch Girald.

There was a small chapel guarded by several dozen

men-at-arms in a mixture of baronial liveries, but they made no move to stop us as we walked towards the door. Inside we found their masters. Clifford lay bandaged with a priest at his side; Earl Thomas and Mowbray were praying at the altar.

Harclay walked straight up to them.

"Forgive me for breaking in on your prayers," he said, "but the truce is over."

Earl Thomas stood up slowly and turned to us with a face that was scowling and colourless.

"May you roast in hell for this, Harclay," he said, drawing his sword from its scabbard and throwing it onto the stone floor at our feet.

Chapter Twelve

THE WHEEL SPINS

WORD OF THE BATTLE reached York before we did, and when we rode in that evening they lit the streets with torches in our honour. There was cheering and singing, and the rich merchants leaned out of their windows to watch us pass. A girl threw Harclay a garland of primroses, and one or two of the townsfolk aimed a clod of filth at Earl Thomas. Even the bells of the Minster were rung in celebration. You would never have known it was Lent.

The further we rode, the wilder the crowds became, grasping at Harclay as though he were St. Francis, while pots and stones came flying through the air at the rebels. By the time we reached the castle Harclay had had his gloves pulled from his hands and his spurs stolen and Earl Thomas was spattered with muck.

Archbishop William was waiting at the foot of the stairway that stretched up the great mound to the keep.

"How are the mighty fallen," he said wryly.

Earl Thomas made no reply, but then he had not uttered a word since he cursed Harclay in the chapel at Boroughbridge. He was led away by Sir Simon Ward, not towards the keep with its firelit hall but across the yard, towards the dungeons.

"The people are glad to see him tumble," said Harclay. "It must be all those years that he rode around like a king while they were starving."

Archbishop William stroked his beard. "There is more than hatred in the air tonight," he said. "I have not seen crowds in the streets like that since the days of Edward Longshanks and the last northern victories. It is you they are cheering, Sir Andrew. You are the David who slew Goliath. They are giving you a place in the house of fame."

Harclay shook his head. "Thomas destroyed himself. I was in the right place at the right moment, but that is all."

"Never say that again," warned the Archbishop. "Let it have been the act of a knight crusader. The kingdom needs one."

"I would say it needed at least seven hundred," said Harclay. "What happens to Thomas now?"

"The King is at Pontefract, and bids you deliver the Earl to him there."

"Pontefract?" repeated Harclay, and gave a groan that changed into a laugh. "So he's going to have Thomas judged in the hall of his own castle? Edward never misses a chance to spit."

Seen at twilight from the north-west, Pontefract Castle was like a black crag jutting out of soft hills. Drawing closer, and counting the number of torchlit windows in each of the great round towers, I understood how Thomas had dreamt he was King Arthur.

No sooner had we arrived than Harclay and Sir Simon Ward were ushered into the royal presence and Thomas was hustled down into his own dungeons. The rest of us were left with the ordeal of finding ourselves food and a corner in which to stretch out for the night. The castle was a city in itself, a labyrinth of halls, chambers, passages and stairways, all of them crowded with the people of the royal court and army. I wandered around in a growing distemper until I remembered the one quiet place in Helmsley Castle and headed for the Chapel.

It was lit by two candles that burned on the altar, and deserted but for a boy who was praying on the altar steps. As I approached, he rose and turned towards me, making me gasp and step backwards. It was the dwarf I had last seen running away from the burning library at Fountains.

"I know you," I said shakily. "You set fire to our abbey."

The wrinkled little man staring up at me was as terrified as I was.

"It is true," he said, in a voice that was deep and dignified. "Earl Thomas ordered me to. How could I refuse?"

"You are his servant?" I asked, arching my eyebrows and hoping I looked like an inquisitor.

He twirled on his toes and gave a low bow. "I am Roland," he replied, "jester, juggler, minstrel, reader of the tarot, and servant of any lord who makes me welcome." He swung upright and looked at me solemnly. "Earl Thomas made me welcome, and the only service he ever asked of me was one or two deeds which were his will but beneath his dignity as a knight."

"So you burnt our library to please him?" I asked incredulously. "I would say a servant can be judged by the master he chooses."

"Can he?" asked the dwarf with a smile. "I am only as guilty as my master, Earl Thomas, if you are as pure as your master, St. Bernard. Surely we both know how easy it is to hide inside another man's rule?"

I could find no answer to that. "Why were you not with Earl Thomas at Boroughbridge?" I asked.

"Because I have no desire to die for him," said Roland. "I watched his Fortune ebbing away, and I knew long before he ran for Scotland that the pageant was over. I was not the only one who chose his moment to fade into the shadows."

"So you were following not Earl Thomas but the Wheel of Fortune?" I said.

"Only monks and peasants can afford not to," he said sadly. "Now if you will excuse me, I will bid you goodnight."

He hurried out and left me alone in the chapel, where looking around me I felt a twinge of Bernardine revulsion at the opulence of the painted panels.

In the morning, Harclay brought me writing materials he had begged from one of the chancery scribes.

"I want a plain chronicle, and no fancifying," he ordered. "Write down the banners that were unfurled against us in each charge, and the words that were spoken on the bridge."

So I shut myself in the chapel and scratched away with pen and knife, reliving the horrors of the wicked day and reducing them to a few cold lines of ink. They covered no more than three sheets of parchment, which I carried rolled neatly in one hand when the next morning, at the hour of Terce, Harclay and I climbed the stairway into the keep to attend the court of the King's justice.

The dais of the great hall was lined with empty chairs and faced by three desks where clerks sat ready to record the proceedings. The rest of the hall was a gossiping throng of knights and courtiers who only hushed when the doors behind the dais were opened and the magnates entered in procession. Two of the barons I recognised by their coats-of-arms: Aymer de Valence, the crusty old Earl of Pembroke, who had stood by Edward through thick and thin, and swarthy Earl Warenne, who had stood by Edward because he hated Earl Thomas. Both wore looks of grim satisfaction, as though they were doing something they had been promising themselves for a long time. Then came several bishops, led by John of Norwich, the Lord Chancellor, and in their wake came the King himself.

My first glimpse of Edward of Caernarvon took me by surprise. He was tall and broad-shouldered, and walked with an erectness and poise that took one's eyes straight up his spine to the crown on his head. His long red hair and beard had been meticulously curled into ringlets, and he wore a long scarlet gown on which the Three Lions were embroidered in gold. His grandeur surprised me because all my life I had listened to the tales of his lucklessness and depravity, and had ended up imagining him as horribly deformed. He wore his reputation in a subtler way, in the shape of the slim young man in a doublet of silver-studded velvet who walked two paces ahead of him carrying his sword, and who could only be Hugh Despenser.

The King seated himself at the centre of the dais and raised a jewelled hand. "Bring in the accused," he ordered.

Earl Thomas was led in wearing the same dirt-spattered clothes in which he had surrendered to us at Boroughbridge, and with his wrists chained together behind his back. He swayed on his feet as the guards halted him in the middle of the floor, then he caught sight of Edward and stiffened into his old posture of arrogance. They had not set eyes on each other since the Parliament of Westminster nine months before, and now Edward quivered at the lips with a smile of triumph and Thomas glared back his refusal to accept himself humbled before the man he loathed.

John of Norwich handed the King a scroll, and I realised that Edward was going the read the charges himself, so sweet were their words to his ears.

"This court is summoned to hear the charge of treason that is brought against Thomas, Earl of Lancaster, Lincoln, and Derby, Steward of the Realm of England. He is charged with riding with banners unfurled in open rebellion against his anointed King, and of entering into traitorous allegiance with Robert Bruce, who calls himself King of Scotland." Edward handed back the parchment and settled himself into his chair. "Let the hearing of the witnesses begin."

It was a lengthy business. The first to speak was a knight who had answered the Earl's summons to Doncaster and who told how Earl Thomas had incited the magnates to oppose the King with force. Edward listened in fascination, while the clerks scratched away and caught every word. The Castellan of Tickhill told how for three weeks Thomas had laid siege to a castle that flew the banner of Three Lions, then a wool merchant told how Thomas had seized Burton-on-Trent to hold the bridge against the King and burnt the town as he retreated. The chronicle grew more and more shameful until I stopped listening and stood staring from the Earl to the King, feeling the wash of the current of hate that flowed between them. Thomas stood as still as a statue, as if afraid to make the slightest movement in case it were interpreted as a sign of penitence.

Then I felt Harclay's hand on my shoulder and he stepped forward, pulling me with him as he walked out to stand before the dais.

"My liege," he said, "I leave the testimony of what happened at Boroughbridge to a most impartial observer, Brother Robert of the Order of St. Bernard."

The gaze of the King and court came to rest on me and I flushed the colour of a plum, but once I had taken a deep breath and begun to read I forgot myself, and it was simply as if it were my turn to read the meditations in the abbey refectory. I kept my eyes fixed on the parchment, but I sensed the attentive silence of the hall as I repeated the words that had been spoken on the bridge. When the grisly chronicle was over, I stole a look at Earl Thomas. His face was as expressionless as a mask of death.

Edward turned in his seat to let his gaze wander along the faces of the magnates who sat beside him on the dais.

"My lords and prelates," he said, "we declare that these events are manifest and notorious, and admit no right of reply. Would any of you disagree with us?"

No one said a word. Edward glowed with triumph and turned his gaze back at Thomas.

"The accused is guilty of treason, and the penalty for treason is that the traitor be hung, drawn, and quartered." He paused to study his rings, and when he spoke again he spoke slowly, to let every word linger. "As the accused is of noble blood he shall merely be beheaded."

They were the very words that Thomas must have used ten years before when he sentenced Gaveston. Edward was savouring every drop of his goblet of revenge.

The Earl was led out by the guards, and the crowd shuffled impatiently, waiting for the King to rise and the session to end.

"We will close with happier business," declared Edward. "We call on Sir Andrew Harclay."

Harclay walked out into the middle of the floor. "My liege?"

"Sir Andrew, we are most grateful for the service you have given us at a time when men of noble blood have seen fit to betray their King, and your deed of valour will not go unrewarded. We are minded that the nobility might do more honour to the kingdom if their ranks held men like yourself, and to that end we hereby create a new lordship, to be known as the Earldom of Carlisle, and we bestow it upon you."

Harclay looked utterly taken aback. "But my liege," he protested. "I have no lands. I am only fit to be a knight . . ."

Edward held up a hand to silence him. "Naturally you think at once of your responsibilities. From the estates that will shortly be forfeited by the rebels, we will grant you a domain fit for an earl. So be wondrous no longer; accept and rejoice."

Harclay dropped to his knees and placed his hands between the King's, and I found I was rubbing my eyes. I had just seen the Wheel of Fortune in spin, hurling Earl Thomas down to his end in the same moment that it lifted Andrew Harclay to the beginnings of power and fame.

Next day I joined the crowds who braved the rain to stand on the battlements and watch Earl Thomas ride out to his death.

As the last drop of his revenge for Gaveston, the King had ordered the execution to take place on a bare hilltop a short distance from the castle, forcing Thomas to run the gauntlet of a jeering crowd of soldiers and peasants. He was led out mounted on the scraggiest mare I had seen in all our years of famine, and dressed in the white robe of a penitent. Bareheaded in the rain, unable to protect himself from the clods of mud that came flying from the crowd, he somehow kept his pride to the bitter end.

A hand tugged at my sleeve and I looked down to see Roland the dwarf standing beside me.

"Are you going to put this in your chronicle?" he asked sarcastically. "Will you say that from a height it looked the way it must have looked when Christ was led out from Jerusalem?"

"No," I said. "There will be no more chronicles."

A group of churchmen came walking past us, and I was startled when John of Norwich stopped and offered me his ring to kiss.

"I was impressed by your chronicle of Boroughbridge," he said. "In my chancery we have need of scribes of your abilities, and I should like to make you the offer of a living."

"Your Grace is most generous," I replied, "but I can only follow St. Bernard in the silence of the wilderness."

"As you wish," said the Bishop, with mild surprise. "May God be with you."

He swept away along the rampart, leaving Roland shaking his head in disbelief.

"You must have a brain full of curd," he said. "That was the Wheel of Fortune itself, stopping in front of you to let you reach out and grasp it, and all you do is cover your face and whimper about St. Bernard. I have never seen anything so pitiful in all my life."

"I know," I said, "but the more I know about the Wheel the more I hate it. I could never make it my quest."

"Quest?" repeated the dwarf. "Who said anything about quests? Perhaps you had better run back to your cloister before the world dirties you with life?"

"Yes," I agreed, and walked away as fast as my legs could carry me. I searched the castle until I found Harclay, who was surrounded by a ring of effusive courtiers.

"Release me from your service" I begged him.

"You cannot leave me now," he protested gaily. "An earl needs a scribe. Let me write to Abbot Walter . . ."

"You have the chronicle you asked me for," I cut in. "Three days from now it is the Feast of the Annunciation, and I should like to be back at the abbey in time for it."

Harclay shrugged. "Have it your own way. Take the horse you have been riding and keep it in the abbey stables until I have a chance to send for it." He reached for his belt-pouch. "Let me give you some money for the journey."

"No," I all but shouted at him. "You can keep your thirty pieces of silver for yourself."

Chapter Thirteen

THE PAST

ONE WARM EVENING at the end of September, Abbot Walter asked me to join him for a walk through the orchards and gardens that lay downstream of the abbey. We had the paths to ourselves, and as we walked I rubbed a sprig of lavender between my fingers and breathed in the last lingering scents of the summer.

"What is your favourite herb?" asked the Abbot.

I looked at the rows and rows of plants brought from every land in the world and blushed. "Forgive me, Father, but I know so few of them by name that I cannot say."

"There is still time," said the Abbot. "Twenty is no great age. You are still at the doorway of life and learning." He ran a finger lightly over his cheek to brush off a fly. "Let me see, it must be five months since you returned from Pontefract?"

"Yes, Father."

"And how have those five months seemed to you?"

I hesitated. It had been a mellow spring. The catkins and coltsfoot had come early, and so had Scottish raiding and the heavy taxes to give the King an army to march north with. Then there had been the golden summer, the richest wool clip in years, and the mercy of a fine harvest.

"There is much to rejoice about," I replied.

"We would never have guessed that from your face," said Abbot Walter gently. "To us you have seemed very distant.

You go about your work and your devotions like a sleep-walker. It is as if you are here in body but not in spirit."

His words were like a gust of wind on the dust of thoughts in the corners of my mind. All at once I was tongue-tied with fear of saying anything that might offend him.

"What is it?" he asked. "Confess your thoughts."

"It is not what I think but where my mind goes," I said, fumbling for words. "It is so peaceful here, with our ordered days and our ordered gardens, but somehow my thoughts never fly upwards to God. They fly sideways, out into the world, and I find myself wondering what is happening to the people I met on my travels. Even when I'm kneeling in the choir I think about them."

"And you wish that you were with them?"

"Sometimes I long to be, but then I remember that the world is a nightmare, and it fills me with fear just to think of it. But here . . ."

"Here you do not feel alive," said the Abbot softly.

I nodded so quickly that he laughed with embarrassment, but his eyes were full of love.

"You are caught between two worlds, Robert, and at the moment you belong in neither of them. You have loved too sharply beyond these walls. Sometimes a man who has spent his life in the world can turn, when the meat of his years are gone, and devote those that remain to God, often with far greater zeal than one of the Meek who has known a vocation since childhood; but for you it is too early. Your life is still unresolved. You will not find the answers here, and you will never belong here until they are found."

"But I try," I protested. "I live by the Rule. I know I have broken it in the past . . ."

"You live by the Rule, and every day you die a little," said Abbot Walter. "That is now how it is meant to be." We had reached the orchards, where the air was heavy with the scent of apples. "I could let you make your vows," he said. "I could watch you labour away the spring and summer of your life over the scrolls in the muniment room. You would do it, out of duty to us, duty to your father, and fear of the world, and I could watch you become a barren husk of a man with less soul than a handful of last year's harvest."

"What are you saying?" I asked. "Are you sending me away?"

"I'm sending you back where you came from. If your father had not sent you here you would have grown up to be a squire. Go to Earl Andrew of Carlisle. Ask to be his squire, or use what you have learnt here and become his scribe. Find your own way, and it will take you wherever you are meant to go, but I believe you know in your heart that your way is not the way of the cloister."

"But how can I find the Earl?" I protested. "He must be somewhere in Scotland with the King."

Abbot Walter shook his head. "I happen to know he is at Knaresborough, less than a day's ride from here." He laid his hands on mine. "At Compline, I will tell the brothers you are leaving."

I followed him speechlessly back towards the abbey.

In the morning the master of novices took away my cassock and cowl and gave me strange clothes: a woollen doublet and leg-hose that had been made on one of our granges, and an ancient long green cloak fastened with a silver clasp that must have gone out of fashion when my father was a boy. The hose made my legs feel both hot and naked at the same time. Feeling like a stranger to myself I teetered out into the cellarer's yard where the rounsey Harclay had lent me in the spring was saddled and waiting. I paused to press my cheek against the warm brown stone of the abbey, and when Brother Ambrose hurried out to give me a bag of writing materials and food, we folded into each other's arms.

"My dear boy," he murmured, thumping me on the back

as though I had hiccups. "Remember me whenever you eat a venison pasty. They are the only things I miss."

It was turning into a hot morning, so like the day on which I had first ridden up to the abbey eight years before. I wondered where I was placed on the Wheel of Fortune.

A wide river swept along the rocky bed of a wooded gorge, looking so much like the Swale at Richmond that I caught my breath at the pang of memories.

As at Richmond, the highest cliff of the gorge was crowned with a castle, but there the likeness ended, for Knaresborough was no grizzled stronghold going back to the days of the Conqueror. It soared upwards in bright new stonework, a high curtain wall with circular towers curling round the clifftop into a massive keep that looked a fortress in itself. From the highest turret flew a blue banner emblazoned with a white hawk, which made me shake my head and laugh aloud. For years it had been no more than a badly-painted design on Harclay's shield, and now it was the banner of the Earl of Carlisle.

The gatehouse was guarded by men-at-arms who wore the blue and white hawk badge sewn onto their jerkins. One of them recognised me and waved me through into a yard filled with stables which stank as only castle yards on a hot day know how to stink. I dismounted quickly and hurried through a second gatehouse into an inner ward where at least the air was kinder.

The Earl, a steward informed me, was out hunting, so I searched around the yard until I found some shade in which to sit and wait. Harclay rode in towards evening, took one look at me and burst out laughing.

"Robert! Where on earth did you get those clothes?"

"I have come to ask to be your squire," I replied, wondering if an earl were 'my liege' or 'my lord'.

"And does the good Abbot Walter know that you have run away from the cloister?"

"I did not run away. He told me to leave."

At this Harclay laughed even louder and clapped me on the shoulder. "Fair enough. Anyone God rejects can find service with me. You can write the chronicle of my knightly adventures."

There was a loud gaiety about him that reminded me unpleasantly of Earl Thomas, or even of Girald de Ros. I wondered if it were a ritual bearing that lords were meant to adopt.

With a swagger to his step and an arm around my shoulders Harclay led me up into the great hall of the keep. Servants wearing his emblem were scurrying around setting the tables for supper, and I let out a whistle of wonder at the tall arched windows which lit each end of the hall.

"You have a fine castle," I said breathlessly.

Harclay took a goblet of wine and drained it in two long gulps. "Not only is it fine, Robert, it is rare," he said, wiping his lips and passing the goblet to a page to be refilled. "You are standing in the only castle in all England that has been built by order of Edward of Caernarvon. His father built them everywhere – he covered Wales with them and had his son born in the finest of them all – but our good King has built only one in all his life."

"Well," I said cheerily, "it is magnificent. This keep is a fortress in itself."

"It had to be. It was a gift for Piers Gaveston." Harclay fixed me with his grey eyes and there was no hiding the merriment in them. "So you see how high I stand in the favour of the King." He laughed yet again. "Eat well, Robert. Afterwards we will talk."

The meal was a procession of dishes fit for a magnate: hares in civey with an almond brewet, roast coneys and capons with a brown herbolace, salmon pasties with savoury rice; and the wine flowed like a river. Every time I looked at Harclay, he was drinking. The clatter was so loud I could not hear a word anyone said to me, so I nodded or grinned and soon they left me alone, which was just as well as the food was giving me quite enough to think about. It was so long since I had eaten roast fowl that I had forgotten where the bones were.

As we finished with pears and peeled medlars, a small figure jumped up onto the tables and began to play on a lute. It was none other than Roland the dwarf, resplendent in a blue doublet emblazoned with the white hawk, and the song he sang was of Eleanor of Aquitaine. I was listening entranced when Harclay rose and signalled to me to follow him.

We climbed the stairs to an ornate chamber with richly-carved chairs, a bed with tapestried hangings, and with its own fireplace set into the wall of the keep. Outside it was gathering dusk. A page came in with wine, while another closed the shutters and kindled us a fire of juniper logs. When they had gone, Harclay settled himself into the chair nearest to the fire and told me to pull up the other.

He left the wine to stand untouched, and in the firelight his face changed, getting older as the shadows collected in the wrinkles around his eyes. He sat with his head back and his nostrils flared to catch the tang of the juniper, and when at length he spoke it was in the dry, measured voice that I remembered.

"You did the right thing the day you left Pontefract. There were twenty-five executions before Edward calmed down, and I've lost count of the number who were murdered in dungeons or shut away to rot."

He shivered at the memory of it.

"Is that why you are not with the King of Scotland?" I asked.

"Oh no," he said, and smiled. "Nothing so noble, though you are not far from the truth. I was summoned to the council to discuss the course to be taken by the King's campaign in Scotland. They listened to my advice and ignored every word of it."

He pointed to the wine, so I filled us each a goblet and drank when he drank. Every so often he glanced at me to make sure I was listening, but mostly he avoided my eyes and talked to the flames. I wondered how many years it was since he had last been to confession.

"I could hardly believe it," he said. "Pembroke and Arundel served up the same turkey they've been stuffing all their lives – offer money to everyone in England who can walk and swarm north like a plague of locusts. Holy Mary! It worked twice for Edward Longshanks twenty years ago and has failed every time we've tried it since. There is no way to feed an army like that off the land. There was at first, but not any more. All you can do is crawl north like an overweight snail, giving the Scots time to strip the country ahead of you of everything except the rabbits. And Robert Bruce does not ride out to give battle in polished armour and jingling spurs; he melts into the hills and hits you in the darkness just where you least want to meet him. Honestly, eight years and the thrill of killing Thomas are all it takes for them to forget the truth about the valley of the Bannockburn."

He paused to drink.

"Did you say all that to them?" I asked.

"With as much patience as I could find. Pembroke turned sulky and suggested I tell them how I would conquer Scotland. So I told them." Harclay reached forward to settle some more logs on the fire. "I told them it was over. I told them to recognise Bruce as the lawful King of Scotland and ask for Berwick in exchange. They were not amused, and that is why they left me behind. Edward named me Warden of the Marches, and Pembroke hissed that mine would be the blame if a single Scot set foot in the realm while they were away. I should not be speaking ill of them; they may be dead by now."

"How long have you known this?" I asked. "About Scotland?"

"Years," he said wearily. "Since Edward of Caernarvon came to the throne, long before the castles started falling, long before the valley of the Bannockburn. Your father knew it from the very beginning."

"My father?" I repeated wonderingly. "Why did he serve all those years in the garrison at Stirling if he knew there was no hope?"

Harclay nodded. "I wanted to ask him that very question, but Stephen was a hard man to get to talk about himself. Now I wonder if it was out of love for Longshanks. Perhaps he was haunted by that one time he went against Edward's will?"

"How?" I asked. "What did he do?"

"Think, Robert. Think of your mother."

I tried to unlock my memories and found there were none. "No one at Richmond ever spoke of her."

Harclay gave me a look of disbelief which faded as he saw my bewilderment. "Good God," he said. "Do you really not know?"

"Tell me," I pleaded.

He refilled my goblet and sat back with his own.

"You have seen my rise, Robert. I am a landless knight who watched which way the wind blew and turned up in the right place at the right moment to earn my reward. Well, Stephen was a landless knight, but he was also the only man I have ever met who lived his chivalry. He served Longshanks with a loyalty so pure it was almost love. They rode on crusade together; they rode together through the conquest of Wales; and when the Scottish quarrel came to war and Edward rode north with more old man's anger than sense, your father was the first to ride with him." Harclay smiled into his wine. "Then Stephen fell in love. He was like a knight who had finally found his quest, and when Edward ordered him to throw the girl out, he told the King he would not obey."

"But why was the King so angry?" I asked.

"Your mother's name was Katherine," said Harclay. "Katherine Bruce."

I almost dropped my goblet.

"From the Bruces of Skelton, not of Annandale, but kin nonetheless, and that is why your father ended his life a landless knight in the service of Count John of Richmond. Edward never spoke to him again. Then your mother died, and it was not long after that that Stephen rode north to join the garrison of Stirling. Perhaps he thought it was as good a place as any to be lonely?"

"He could have taken me with him," I protested.

"Could he?" asked Harclay. "To watch you grow up wanting to be a knight? It would have been more than he could bear. The Scottish war cured a lot of us of our belief in chivalry, and Stephen's must have been the hardest cure of all. In his heart he was almost a Templar."

The door to another chamber of my memory swung open: I saw Harclay pulling open the rough leather jerkin of the murdered knight and staring at the red cross on a white surcoat.

"The Knights Templar," I murmured. "You never did tell me who they were."

"I shouldn't have to," said Harclay, suddenly tossing the dregs of his wine into the flames and making the fire hiss like a cat. "They were the finest knights the world has ever seen," he said softly, "an order whose vow was the guarding of the Holy Land for Christendom. It was a sacred purpose, a torch of chivalry that was handed down from generation to generation . . ." Harclay grimaced. "God! Already the words sound hollow. The Templars changed, of course. They became so rich they were the envy of Kings, but they were still the guardians of the heart of Christendom."

"What happened?" I asked.

"You can read the rest of the story in any chronicle," said Harclay bitterly. "The tide of Saracens became too great, and the Templars alone could not stop them. It would have needed a crusade of all Christendom. So the Holy Sepulchre fell, and the Templars fled the Holy Land. They were still rich, with castles in every country, but their purpose had been lost. It was soon after that that the persecution started."

"So Girald de Ros merely joined in the hunt?"

"Like any other jackal." Harclay looked at me curiously. "By the way, what is your quarrel with Girald? Has it anything to do with that scar round your face?"

"It is not a good story," I said quickly.

"I'll decide that," he said, and poured us more wine.

So I stared into the fire and relived it all in the mirror of the flames, and for the first time I saw it from a distance, and for the first time it was not a confession, just a tangled chronicle of hope and failure.

When I finished, Harclay shook his head several times and laughed softly.

"By God, you are Stephen's son." He rolled his eyes. "The enchantment of love, stirring knights to noble deeds; and there was I thinking stories like that belonged to the past."

"They do," I said. "That is what I learnt. All I did only made things worse. I do not deserve to wear her ring."

"To be true you must wear it always," said Harclay dreamily. "You must be faithful, even if your quest lasts for years." He snapped back into a laugh. "At least, that is how it would have been in the past."

I hung my head. It was all too late.

"Go to bed, Robert," said Harclay.

Swaying to my feet I felt the gathered power of the wine, and my mind swirled with sadness.

"Damn Edward Longshanks!" I cursed. "Damn all those years my father was alone at Stirling."

Harclay sprang from his chair and shook me by the shoulders.

"Never pity Stephen. Always remember that you are the proof he had the last laugh on Edward."

"Me?" I asked. "How?"

A wicked glint came into Harclay's eyes. "He named you Robert, just when it was becoming the most unpopular name in England."

Chapter Fourteen

THE RESCUE

I WAS WOKEN by whistling and the glare of sunlight as shutters were thrown open. My head felt like a baked apple. Roland the dwarf was skipping around at the foot of the bed, throwing a blue bundle up into the air and leaping across the room to catch it with his other hand.

"The Earl bids you attend him in the great hall," he announced, and tossed the blue bundle into my lap. It was a doublet emblazoned with the white hawk, tight-fitting and with fastenings at the back which Roland laced up as I tried to rub the sleep from my eyes.

"So you found a new lord," I remarked.

"It seems we both have," he replied. "Let's hope his Fortune is strong enough to carry us."

In the great hall, I found Harclay in conference with his stewards. He grinned at the sight of me wearing his colours.

"Get yourself some mulled wine and cold meat, Robert, then hurry down to the courtyard. We are going to Helmsley."

I blinked blearily. "Truly?"

"Truly," said Harclay. "How can I resist such a noble quest? Besides, my men need the exercise."

"What about Girald?"

"Girald has been an outlaw since the battle of Boroughbridge, and his powerful friends are all dead. I should think we'll find him a changed man."

The bells of Knaresborough Abbey were calling the monks to Mass as we rode out of the castle with an escort of fifty men-at-arms and Roland the dwarf.

It was the first day of October but the land still had the feel of the summer's end; the only signs of autumn were the gilt on the beech leaves and the clusters of red berries on the rowans. We did not stop until we were past York and deep into the Forest of Galtres, and then only for a few moments to water the horses before pushing on as fast as before. The road was different to the one I remembered, winding through small rounded hills then turning north across wooded slopes to swoop down on Helmsley like a bird of prey.

We thundered through the village, scattering the pigs and hens in all directions, and straight up to the southern gatehouse of the castle. It was barred with the iron grille.

"God's blessing on those within," called Harclay, "and may He grant them the grace to look to their guests."

Someone peered over the battlements at us and bobbed quickly out of sight. We heard footsteps running away, and then there was silence. Harclay beckoned forward some of the archers to flank him. After a while we heard footsteps hurrying up the stairs in the gatehouse and two heads appeared at the battlements. I recognised the plump face of Ralph the steward,

"Who are you?" he called out.

Harclay held up his sword with the blade pointing downwards. "Earl Andrew of Carlisle, the Warden of the Marches, who desires a friendly word with Lord de Ros."

"My apologies," called Ralph, and he turned to buffet the man beside him. "Open up, you fool," he ordered.

The grille was raised and we clattered across the bridges into the castle, just in time to see Ralph puffing up the stairs into the west tower. By the time we had ridden over and dismounted he had reappeared, and with him was Lord

William, who hurried down the steps and gazed at Harclay as though he were the Archangel Michael.

"Sir Andrew, I mean Earl Andrew ..." he exclaimed joyfully.

"I thank you for your gracious welcome," replied Harclay.

"This is an honour indeed," said Lord William. "I trust I can offer you hospitality for the night?"

Harclay gave one of his best smiles of jovial lordship, but he made a point of letting his eyes rove slowly around the castle before replying.

"That pleasure may have to wait until I am less burdened by my duties as Warden of the Marches, but I would be honoured to drink a cup of wine with you."

"An honour I am proud to bestow," said Lord William, and I was beginning to believe him. "If you and your men will join me in my hall ..."

"Five of us will join you. The others will drink their wine out here," said Harclay. He nodded to me and to three of his grisliest men-at-arms, then turned and let Lord William lead him eagerly up the stairs.

The hall was cleaner and the air fresher than I remembered it, as if there had been fewer rowdy nights of late. We were seated at the high table, and Lord William's sickly son was brought in to have the honour of meeting the Earl of Carlisle. In three years the boy had hardly grown an inch, and he had a hollow cough which shook him whenever it came. Lord William waited until we had all been poured wine, then raised his goblet in a toast.

"To King Edward."

"God preserve him," added Harclay. "It is the search for his enemies which brings me here. I was hoping to find your brother, Girald."

"Thankfully I am able to disappoint you," said Lord William. "Girald has not set foot here since the day of his outlawry."

Harclay raised an eyebrow. "And there has been no word from him in over five months?"

Lord William's smile frayed ever so slightly. "There have, I confess, been two messengers who came with his ring to demand money, but there has been no word at all since July." He dropped his gaze to his goblet. "I live in fear of my brother. He is a man who touches everything with evil, and in my heart I hope he will never return."

"Which is why you keep the gate barred," said Harclay. "A wise precaution."

"Girald is a man of many crimes," said Lord William. "In my prayers I ask God for a knight who will rid England of such evil."

"Amen," said Harclay, accepting more wine. "The King will rejoice when he hears of your loyalty. I remember hearing that one of Girald's crimes was to marry a girl against her will and keep her shut up here as a prisoner. Is that true?"

"The poor girl is still here, living proof of my brother's cruelty."

"Then my quest is at an end," said Harclay. "We have come to her rescue."

Lord William paled. "But you cannot! Girald would be enraged."

"He can always come looking for me," said Harclay, "and you can tell him I took her by force." He winked at me. "My squire, Robert de Falaise, will go and prepare the lady for her journey."

"My steward will take him to her," said Lord William unhappily.

Ralph bowed as I rose, a frown crossing his face when he had a good look at mine. He led me silently up the stairs in the west tower to an oak door at the end of a passageway. I waited until he left me before I knocked.

There was no answer. I pushed the door open, wincing as

it groaned on its hinges, and walked into a small bedchamber. Marie was sitting by the window, wearing a gown of holly-green and with her hair bound tightly into a caul. She looked up wearily from her embroidery, screamed, and sprang to her feet with her hands clapped over her mouth.

I ran across the room and took her hands in mine. She was shaking with fright.

"Marie, you are free. I have come back with the Earl of Carlisle and many men. You are free."

She gulped and nodded and stared at me. In three years her face had grown gaunt and lost its softness, but there was a dance of beauty in her eyes and eyebrows that had never been there before. She pulled one of her hands free and lifted it to my face, grimacing as she ran her fingertips along the line of my scar.

"He told me you were dead," she said angrily. "He told me you were buried at Rievaulx."

"Will you come?"

"Oh you idiot," she said. "Do you even need to ask?"

The sun was dipping towards the hills as we mounted up in the yard of the castle. Marie ignored Lord William as she swept down the steps, but she stopped to hug his son, who clung to her tearfully until she kissed him on the forehead and pulled away. Harclay took a long look at her and hurried forward to help her mount.

"Earl Andrew of Carlisle at your service," he murmured gallantly, and as he settled himself onto his own horse he glanced at me with amused eyes and pursed lips.

So we rode out, through the open gates under the white battlements, through the straggle of village and out into the fields beyond. So fast did Harclay pace the cavalcade that I was fearful for Marie, but whenever I glanced at her her head was back and her eyes half-closed in rapture at the wind blowing in her face.

I was resigning myself to a night ride to Knaresborough when Harclay turned off the road and spurred his horse up onto a rounded hilltop. Much of it was pasture, with grass cropped low by sheep, but a wood ran over the crest and gave shelter from the wind. Harclay gave the order to make camp, and when the horses were tethered and the men were crashing about in the trees gathering firewood I wandered over to join Marie, who stood gazing at the view.

North and south of us the hilltops rolled into the distance in wave upon wave, but to our west the Vale of York stretched to the horizon like a green sea. The Forest of Galtres lay below us, with here and there an amber-topped beech tree, and beyond it, like a carved bone chess-piece, was York Minster.

Marie took my hand. "I have never stood on a hilltop before."

"Did Girald punish you?" I asked.

She kept her eyes fixed on the distant city. "The first year was hard, but after that he gave up and left me alone. By then he was too caught up with Earl Thomas, and he had spent all my money, so all he wanted was for me to be shut up and forgotten." She looked at me out of the corner of her eyes. "And what of you? You are not a blushing monk any more. You look as though you've had many adventures."

I kissed her hand. "You are my only adventure. The last three years have been a nightmare, but today has been my rescue."

She rocked on her heels with laughter. "Oh Robert, you still talk like a troubadour."

We were joined by Harclay, who bowed to Marie. "I fear I must ask you to spend a night with few comforts," he said ruefully. "My men are building you a bower out of branches, and we do have blankets. Perhaps tomorrow I will have the honour of feasting you in my castle at Knaresborough?"

"I cannot thank you enough," said Marie. "All I ask tomorrow is an escort to York."

Harclay looked disappointed. "Well, that you shall have. I have sent men down to a grange to get food, and we are kindling a fire just over the brow. Join us there before you get cold."

As he strolled away, Marie shivered.

"What is it?" I asked. "You must not be afraid of Harclay. He is a good man."

"I think I will be afraid of knights for the rest of my life," she said, and pointed to my doublet. "Why are you wearing his coat-of-arms?"

"Because I am proud to," I said. "He gave it to me."

"And it was an open gift?" asked Marie earnestly. "You do not belong to him?"

"I belong only to you."

She laughed again, took my arm, and we set off towards the fire.

The foragers came back laden with chickens, beer, honey cakes and blackberries. The sight of it all made my mouth water. Less than a year before the country had been wailing with famine, and no one had even had the barley to make beer.

"The power of life to renew itself is the holiest of mysteries," I murmured.

Harclay chuckled. "There speaks a monk. Have you ever thought of taking to the cloister?"

The night was warm and starless, and we sat in a wide ring around the fire, ducking whenever it crackled and spat out flakes of bark. Harclay was like Robin of the Wood: sitting on a log with his beer in one hand and a chicken leg in the other he told story after story of the border, calling on this or that man around the fire to back up each tale or to add to it. It was a while before I realised that he was doing it to lift their spirits. In all that was said, there was not one word spoken about King Edward, or of what might or might not be happening on the border even as we sat there.

Marie fell asleep against my shoulder, and with Harclay's help I carried her to the bower and wrapped her round with blankets. As we stood back he gave what was almost a sigh.

"I remembered today how jealous I was when Stephen found his Katherine," he said wistfully. "I envy you."

Without their mask of jollity his eyes stared with loneliness. I tried to find a way of hugging him with words and ended up making a poor jest.

"Surely the Earl of Carlisle is the dream knight of half the maidens in the North?"

"Only half?" he asked, feigning great sorrow. "At least I will always have the vision of you and Marie safe in Aquitaine."

"Thank you for making it your quest," I said.

He shook his head and looked out over the Vale of York.

"Keep the fine words for yourself. It was your inspiration, and I was just the muscle behind another man's will. That is all I have ever been. When I was your age I was sure I would find one noble deed, a deed with a purpose so shining it would be the meaning of my whole life. I gave up searching for it years ago, but today made me wonder what it would have felt like."

Our eyes met and he pulled back inside his mask.

"It also taught me that monks are unused to hard riding. For God's sake get some sleep."

I was woken by the sound of running feet. Men were treading out the embers of the fire and the archers were grabbing their bows and running towards the crest of the hill. In the distance I could hear hoofbeats galloping towards us.

It was almost dawn, and a greyish light was dripping through the clouds. I scrambled up to join Harclay, who was peering down into the murky gloom of the Forest.

"Is it Girald?" I asked.

"Whoever it is, they will have seen our fire from miles away."

He spread us out along the skyline to look as much as possible like an army. Marie came running up with her blankets still wrapped around her, and under the pretence of being manly and protective I clung to her in terror.

A large group of horsemen came thundering out of the Forest and straight up the hillside. Their leader waved to us from his saddle.

"Andrew?" he shouted. "Earl Andrew?"

Harclay gave a groan of relief. "Ride on up, Roger," he called back, and all over the hilltop there were bursts of laughter as our nerves unwound.

The leader of the horsemen was the knight Harclay had left in charge of Knaresborough, and his face was grim.

"Word came from the border yesterday afternoon," he said breathlessly. "Edward is running south. He wants you to meet him at Byland Abbey with every man you can muster."

"Byland?" repeated Harclay, his voice snarling with anger. "He is running all the way to Byland? I suppose he hopes Bruce will burn Northumberland and Durham and forget about him? Holy Jesus!"

He uttered several larger oaths before calming down and looking wearily round the hilltop. "Break the camp," he ordered, and turned to Marie and me. "The road to York will not be safe now. Go back to Helmsley, then you, Robert, join me at Byland. Once we know . . . "

"You are not taking me back to Helmsley," said Marie. "I will not go."

Harclay glared at her. "You must go somewhere safe, and believe me, nowhere in the Vale of York will be safe from the Scots."

"Rosedale Abbey," I suddenly remembered. "The house

of white nuns in the depths of the moors away from everything."

"Thank God for white nuns," said Harclay gratefully. He beckoned to Roland. "You ride with them and keep them out of trouble." Then he kissed Marie's hand and kissed me on the cheek. "Go carefully."

With that he was gone, galloping down the hillside at the head of his men as the dawn broke over the Forest of Galtres.

Chapter Fifteen

THE BLACK BATTLE

ONCE THE RIDERS were gone the stillness returned to the dawn. On a nearby hilltop a flock of birds rose up from some treetops and set off southwards across the sky.

"If only we had wings," I said. "I wonder how soon we could be in Aquitaine?"

"I wouldn't know," said Roland. "I've never flown from here to Aquitaine."

"I should think my Aunt Blanche has," said Marie.

So instead we rode north, through Helmsley where the castle was still asleep and on along the old pilgrims' road to Lastingham. It was nearing midday when we reached St. Cedd's church and called a halt. I watered the horses while Marie washed her face and Roland ran into the village ale-house. He returned with a jug of cider, and as we took turns to drink he peered curiously at Marie and me.

"In the ale-house they say they haven't seen Girald de Ros for months," he remarked. "They also say that Lady de Ros once ran off with a white monk, and that Girald gave the monk a scar to wear for the rest of his life. Am I by any chance looking at a new Abelard and Heloise?"

"Who were they?" I asked.

"Small wonder you don't know," said Roland archly. "Your St. Bernard was no friend of Peter Abelard."

"Abelard and Heloise were two lovers," said Marie softly. "It's a sad story. Let's leave it for another day."

We rode on over the smoke-grey heather of the moors. Towards the hour of Nones we reined back our horses on the rim of Rosedale, looking down on the abbey in its patchwork of green fields.

"It will be better if you ride up alone," I told Marie. "The nuns will make you welcome."

Marie looked at me balefully. "Don't go," she said. "I have a feeling that if you ride off to join Harclay I will never see you again."

"Only Earl Andrew can protect him from your husband," said Roland unhelpfully. "Remember what happened to Abelard."

I told him to shut up and led Marie a short way along the rim of the dale. Roland sat down by the horses and began whistling 'Gather Ye Rosebuds'.

"I must go to Harclay," I explained. "I owe him loyalty, and he is our greatest hope."

Marie nodded unhappily, then flashed her eyes fiercely at me. "Promise me you won't go into battle. Promise me you won't run around trying to be gallant."

"Even if I do face battle, I have your ring to protect me," I said. "All I need now is a kiss."

"Oh Robert," she said reproachfully, "I think I loved you more when you were a monk." But then she slipped her hand round my neck to pull my mouth down to hers, and gave me a kiss which lasted for five Hail Marys and set my heart on fire with longing.

"Do you want to get to Byland before dark or not?" shouted Roland impatiently.

"Wait for me," I begged Marie. "Wait until a month has passed . . ."

"I can wait longer than that," she said. "I know all there is to know about waiting."

So Marie rode down into the dale, and Roland and I turned our horses westwards over the moors.

Hour after hour we rode towards the sun, crossing dale after dale and moor after moor and as lost as friars in the deserts of Tartary. It was pure chance that brought us at sunset to the rim of the Vale of York with just enough light to see a bulging white cliff and a low hill below it which I remembered from the past as lying a few miles north of Byland.

"Say your prayers," said Roland. "Look over there."

Far away to the north a great fire was burning.

"Farmers burning stubble," I said quickly.

"Not in October," said Roland. "That is a town. Somewhere between us and that fire is an army of Scots."

The horses were too spent to gallop, and it was night by the time we turned the low hill and saw the lights of Byland ahead of us. The abbey was ablaze with light, and the great rose window hung in the sky like a glowing Wheel of Fortune. Above it were the stars and beneath it were a hundred camp-fires, scattered among the garths and orchards like candles in a dark church. As we rode towards them we heard laughter and singing, and caught the smell of roasting meat that hung on the wind.

At the first fire we came to the soldiers were as drunk as lords.

"There's a fire to the north," I shouted. "The Scots are coming."

"Hear no evil," yelled a sergeant-at-arms. "We don't want to know and there's nothing we can do about it."

"Where is the Earl of Carlisle?" I asked.

"Over in the abbey with the King," someone shouted.

"Aye, go and spoil their meal," shouted someone else.

I ground my teeth and kicked my horse down the last mile to the abbey, and dismounting in the cellarer's yard I suddenly noticed that Roland had vanished.

Inside the abbey it was like a pageant, with knights and courtiers lolling around in the passageways and the cloister, jesting and japing as the monks moved silently among them with food and wine. I pushed my way to the refectory, where the arched doorway was guarded by men-at-arms who wore the crest of the Three Lions, and peered inside. At the high table sat Edward of Caernarvon, dressed in a purple furred gown and lost in talk with Hugh Despenser, and near them sat Abbot Aylmer with a face of undisguised gloom. A troubadour was singing to them from the reading pulpit. The tables were packed with half the earls and barons of the realm of England, but Harclay was nowhere to be seen.

I grabbed a piece of cheese from a passing monk and began searching for Harclay among the magnates who were crowded in the cloister. As I peered into the faces of the powerful, I was suddenly grabbed by the arm, and spun round to find myself looking up into a face I knew all too well.

"Well met, Brother Scarface," said Girald de Ros.

He was smiling at me. His face had thinned and there were bags under his eyes, and his yellow surcoat was frayed and dirty.

"Have no fear," he said merrily. "I know better than to kill anyone belonging to the Earl of Carlisle."

"I heard you were an outlaw," I said squeakily.

"So I was," he said, "until the King needed soldiers so badly that royal pardons started flying around."

"And the Wheel of Fortune spun you up again?"

Girald winced as though the words had been an insult. "No," he said bleakly, "I would say it dragged me down."

"Into the favour of the King?"

"To being in the King's debt," he said. "To being the one Edward and Despenser get to do their dirty work."

"I should have thought that would come naturally to you," I said, and waited for Girald to hit me.

To my surprise he let go of my arm and leaned back against one of the pillars of the cloister arcade. "Do you think I am evil, Brother Scarface?" he asked, his face hidden in the shadows. "Will you hear my confession and tell me how evil I am?"

"If you wish," I said uneasily.

"What if I told you I had plundered the abbeys of Melrose and Holyrood, and burned the monastery at Dryburgh to the ground, and all on the orders of Edward our King? Does that make me evil?"

I stared at him in horror.

"It makes everything else look small, does it not?" he asked mockingly. "And mark my words, it takes a lot to make my life look small. It even makes the trick you played on me with my wife look like nothing."

Even as he spoke we heard shouting outside the abbey, and high above our heads the bells rang out the alarm.

"The Scots," I said, "they are coming for you."

Girald laughed and pressed himself against the pillar as men ran past and panic spread through the cloister.

"How thoughtful of them," he said. "I must go and get my men on the road to Helmsley. I cannot miss the perfect moment for my homecoming, when my dear family will be so frightened they will let me back in." He stepped out of the shadows and patted me gaily on the shoulder. "Till we meet again, Brother Scarface."

As soon as he had gone I slumped down against the cloister arcade, suffering a strange fit in which I shivered and giggled both at once.

When I came to my senses the cloister was almost empty. Stumbling out into the cellarer's yard I found it full of royal servants who were hastily loading carts. In the moonlight I saw soldiers running from the camp-fires towards a low hill, the brow of which looked to be seething with men. Somewhere among them would be Harclay.

To get there I had to run through the abbey orchards, and in the moonlight they were a fearful place. Groups of men were moving through the trees in all directions, and there was no telling who they were. Feeling like a mouse under a swooping owl I sped on up the open hillside and did not pause for breath until I reached the brow and the crush of men gathered round the banner of Three Lions.

From the hilltop I saw a scene straight out of hell. The northern plains of the Vale of York were pock-marked with the fires of burning villages. Somewhere a church-bell was ringing wildly. In barn after barn the precious harvest was going up in smoke.

Edward of Caernarvon stood by his father's banner, looking down on the battle that was raging below him. In the moonlight there was no way of telling the difference between Englishman and Scot; there were only hundreds of tiny figures who looked like bees swarming around a branch. I scrambled down the hillside from tree to tree until I was within a stone's throw of the carnage, but even from close by it was impossible to see anyone clearly. There was a sound like tearing parchment and an arrow thudded into a tree beside me where it hummed like a harp-string. I decided to get away as fast as my legs could carry me.

Up on the hilltop there was open panic. The archers were now firing volleys down three of the flanks, and the battle-swarm was moving steadily upwards. I ran, slid and slithered down the last open flank, and I was only one of a crowd who were throwing down their weapons and running for the abbey. As I panted through the orchards I heard horsemen behind me and ducked under a tree just as a cavalcade thundered by led by the King and Hugh Despenser. They rode straight past the abbey and on towards the south.

When I reached the cellarer's yard my horse had gone. For a moment I swayed around dreamily, watching the army in full flight down the road towards the Forest of Galtres, then I gathered my wits and turned away, running past the smouldering camp-fires towards the black edge of the moors.

Chapter Sixteen

THE MIRACLE

IT WAS LIKE crawling out of the pit of hell. The higher I climbed the more fires I could see when I looked back, yet the moment I reached the moors I entered a domain of silence, where there was only the inky path through dark trees and grey pastures. The battle was no longer around me but inside me, in the fear that kept me running long after I knew I had lost the path.

When at last I staggered to a halt, I was in a thicket of hazel and blackthorn where the soft ground sucked at my feet, in a shallow wild valley, and utterly lost. When Roland and I had ridden west from Rosedale we had crossed valley after valley and felt we were going against the grain of the land, but we had seen nowhere like this. Eventually I set off downstream, not knowing if every step were taking me back to Byland. I stared up at the stars and thought of all the astronomy books I had leafed through in abbey libraries, searching for a reference to the True Wheel and never stopping to learn the patterns of the night sky.

Soon I fell into a kind of sleep, dreaming of Marie and walking for the touch of her ring that came with each step, and then I came awake and saw everything around me with a piercing clarity: the roots that looked like veins in the earth, the fresh tracks of wild animals, and the flat shadowy skyline ahead that puzzled me until I realised it was the far side of a great dale into which my valley was flowing like a stream into the sea.

Then I was back in a human world of fields and stone walls, and found a line of stepping-stones that carried me across the river to a road that ran down the dale. Looking upstream I saw a cluster of farm buildings, and turning downstream I saw the white walls and arched windows of the Abbey of Rievaulx. All my fear came back. At any moment the monks would be waking up, ringing the bells of Prime and bringing the Scots swarming like ants to honey . . .

I banged on the abbey doors until they were opened by a sleepy Brother Jacob.

"Brother Robert," he exclaimed, then frowned at the sight of my clothes. "What brings you here?" he asked suspiciously.

"I am only a messenger," I said breathlessly. "Take me to Abbot Oswald, and for the love of Our Lady please don't ring any bells."

We burst into the Abbot's chamber where I poured out my warning while Abbot Oswald sat up in bed, his white hair tousled by the pillow into strange tufts like the straws of a scarecrow. When I had finished he turned serenely to Brother Jacob.

"Ring the bells as ever," he said, "but warn the brothers and send Gilbert up to the tower to keep watch. Oh, and bring me a novice's cassock for our guest. Until the storm is past he will be safer as one of us."

Brother Jacob hurried out.

"You must be mad," I protested. "If you ring the bells . . ."

"What will be will be," said Abbot Oswald.

So I told him what the King's army had done to Melrose, and Holyrood, and Dryburgh.

"May God have mercy on their souls," said the Abbot, and opened a window to take a deep breath of fresh air.

"Father," I said imploringly, "you must not let it happen here."

"Brother Robert," he said gently, "all we have is our life of prayer and our obedience to the Rule. They are our only weapons. All we can do is meet the worst of the world with the best of ourselves, and hope that in so doing we plant a seed of good that will flourish when the harvest of evil is past."

"Living in a cloister can make you forget just how evil the world can be," I pointed out.

The Abbot wagged a finger at me. "Never forget that Christ was born in troubled times in a troubled land. He seems, if you will forgive a pun, to have risen to the challenge."

I gave up: you cannot argue with men like Abbot Oswald. Brother Jacob came back with a cassock folded over his arm.

"It is almost daybreak," he said. "Further up the valley there are palls of smoke."

Abbot Oswald took the cassock and offered it to me. "Well Robert, you are welcome to join us."

I nodded and lifted my arms in the air while Brother Jacob unlaced Harclay's doublet and pulled it over my shoulders, then I took the cassock and felt the familiar rub of the coarse wool as I put it on. At least when the Scots came I would be where my father had wanted me to be.

Joining the monks in their choir I felt as if I were stepping back into my past, yet it was only three days since I had left the Abbey of Fountains. The words of the office of Prime came unbidden to my lips; my voice joined the chant while my eyes went to the high double-arched windows with their slender pillars and quatrefoil tracery, and I breathed in the incense that hung in the air.

We were singing when the doors behind us were thrown open and we heard laughter and the sound of breaking glass. I tried to keep my eyes on the altar and my voice on the song but as the Scots ran up the nave and encircled the choir my throat went dry and I began to cough. Some of the brothers kept on singing. A huge Scot with arms like haunches of mutton raised an axe and swung it down onto a lectern, splitting the wood and sending a bible thumping to the floor in a thin cloud of dust. The singing stopped.

"God's greeting to you," said Abbot Oswald to the man with the axe.

"We want you outside," he said. "All of you, and now, not tomorrow."

Abbot Oswald bowed meekly, turned to the altar and crossed himself, then walked towards the door that led out into the cloister yard. The rest of us were herded after him like sheep and pushed into the centre of the yard where the Scots prodded us into a circle with the tips of their weapons. Above us we could hear an axe at work on the door of the abbey treasury.

The huge Scot looked over his shoulder than glared at us. "On your knees," he shouted. "Down on your knees before the King of Scotland."

We sank to the ground and gazed open-mouthed at the middle-aged man who was walking towards us.

Like Edward of Caernarvon, Robert Bruce was not how I expected him to be. He was small and stout, with sagging cheeks and a beard streaked with grey, and teeth that were crooked and yellow. It was in his eyes, that moved quickly and missed nothing, that I felt the legend of the man who had outwitted Edward Longshanks and routed his son, and who spun the Wheel of Fortune as though it were his own. He was also the nearest thing I had to a kinsman.

"God's greeting to you, Lord Robert," said Abbot Oswald. "We have just been praying for the day you might visit us in peace."

Bruce looked grim. "The prayers of monks are not as strong as they used to be, or have you not heard?"

"We have heard of the atrocities in Scotland," replied the Abbot, "and we pray . . ."

"Then you know what is to happen here," cut in Bruce.

"The crime was not ours," protested the Abbot.

"An eye for an eye," said Bruce. "That is the way it has been; that is the way it will be."

Abbot Oswald fell silent, and I realised he had no more to say. I jumped to my feet and made a desperate attempt at rhetoric.

"If you burn this abbey you will not be avenging Melrose," I said, my mind racing like a cataract, "you will be tearing out the one eye that Melrose has left. It was the brotherhood of Rievaulx who sent monks north to found the brotherhood of Melrose. Would you avenge a child by killing the mother?"

One of the Scots levelled his sword against my neck. Bruce looked darkly at me. "And who might you be?"

"My name is Robert de Falaise."

Bruce's eyes narrowed, then his stare clamped onto me and he studied the lines of my face.

"Well then," he said drily, "we had better make Robert a name with a reputation for justice." He turned to Abbot Oswald. "There will be no killing or burning, this time; but now I know how eager you are to help your brothers at Melrose to rebuild their abbey I know you will not mind giving everything you have. You can start by giving them your clothes."

All around the cloister, the Scots roared with laughter as Abbot Oswald bent forward, pulled his cassock up over his shoulders and folded it neatly into a bundle. One by one we did the same until we were standing there as naked as the day we were born, and I could look down and see the green jasper of Marie's ring dangling aginst my chest. Bruce took a last amused look at us and walked out of the abbey, but his men kept a ring of guards around us while they finished their pillaging.

"Is that true about the Abbey of Melrose?" asked Brother Jacob.

"Indeed it is," said the Abbot, looking at me curiously. "But how did you know it was founded by monks from Rievaulx?"

"I read it in the chronicles of your library, one morning three years ago."

"And the Holy Spirit reminded you," said the Abbot triumphantly.

The brothers gathered round to pat me on the back, and as their chatter came at me from all directions, my head began to spin. I was falling asleep on my feet.

When the Scots had gone I was put to bed in the infirmary, where I slept away the day and most of the night. In the morning it was Abbot Oswald himself who brought my breakfast.

"Last night we had word from Byland," he said. "The Earl of Carlisle was there yesterday morning, after the battle, and he was asking if anyone had seen a youth called Robert de Falaise."

"Thank God," I said gratefully, then I remembered Girald.

"Several strays have been found on our granges," said the Abbot, "so we can offer you a horse to go in search of your master. Is there anything else you need?"

"Yes Father, your counsel," I replied, and told him the story of all that had happened since I left the Abbey of Fountains. "What should I do?" I asked him. "Go to Marie in Rosedale, or go to Harclay for protection?"

"It seems to me," he said cautiously, "that de Ros is the kind of man who will come after you. You have struck at his pride, which I suspect is one of the few things he truly cares for. I advise you to go to Earl Andrew, and go quickly. For my part I will find a quiet way of sending a messenger to

Rosedale Abbey so that your lady knows you are alive and well."

So I pulled on my itchy woollen hose, and the Abbot laced me back into Harclay's blue doublet.

We walked together through the abbey. Monks dressed in threadbare clothes and blankets were clearing up the wreckage. Doors had been hacked from their hinges and windows broken. The Scots had even taken the thin marble columns which flanked the doorways of the refectory and chapter house.

"So much has gone," I said sadly.

"Nothing has gone," said the Abbot. "It has been a purification. We are once again the way we were when we came here."

Brother Jacob was waiting for us, holding the reins of a well-bred palfrey with a saddle worthy of a knight.

"How can I ever thank you?" I asked them.

"By returning one day," said Abbot Oswald, "and not bringing trouble with you."

I knelt to receive his blessing.

The Abbey of Byland was a sorry sight. The cellarer's block and lay brothers' range had been burnt, and the whole west front of the abbey had been stained black by the smoke. As I tethered my horse to the remains of the Galilee porch two monks came out to greet me, and at the sight of the white hawk emblazoned on my doublet they grinned from ear to ear.

"God's greeting to you," said the elder of them, "but you have come too late. We have already heard the joyful news."

"What news?" I asked.

"The peace," he replied. "The peace the Earl of Carlisle has made with Robert Bruce."

A few moments later I was hearing the full story from Abbot Aylmer.

"When Earl Andrew left here yesterday morning," he told me, "he dismissed his men-at-arms and rode alone in search of Robert Bruce. They met, they talked, and agreed a settlement by which all English claims to the Scottish throne are to be dropped and six lords from each kingdom are to meet in Newcastle in the spring to seal the treaty in writing. By yesterday evening the Scots were riding north, and today the land is free of them."

"It's a miracle," I said dizzily.

"Yes indeed," said the Abbot, "a fulfilment of all our hopes. Archbishop William had already sent out letters telling all churches to disregard the King's war and sue directly with the Scots for peace, but it needed a magnate to make peace for the whole realm, and for Earl Andrew to act, as Warden of the Marches, is an answer to our deepest prayers."

"What will King Edward do?" I asked warily.

"He has no choice," said Abbot Aylmer. "Once the likes of Earl Andrew make it clear they will no longer live with war on the border, who can the King ask to fight for him?"

"Where is Harclay now?"

"In York. He has ridden there to have the treaty proclaimed."

I set off at once. The road through the Forest of Galtres was littered with the discarded weapons of the fleeing royal army. Where there were dead, the peasants had stripped them of their clothes and left them their armour, giving the road the look of a rubbish pit for men and metal.

It was just after sunset when I reached the city, and the gates had been barred for the night. Looking up at the glow of light in the guardroom of the gate-tower I cleared my throat and shouted.

"Open up in the name of the Earl of Carlisle!"

Footsteps stamped down the stairs and the gate was flung open by a man with a gloomy face who grabbed my bridle as I rode in.

"Keep your voice down, lad," he said darkly. "That's no name to go shouting in the streets."

"Oh yes it is," I said. "You may not want peace but I do. Be so kind as to tell me where the Earl of Carlisle is lodged."

The guard looked at me despairingly. "By now he's probably in the deepest dungeon of the castle. The Earl of Pembroke and Hugh Despenser were waiting for him. He's been proclaimed a traitor of the realm."

Chapter Seventeen

THE RECKONING

THE GUARD WAS KIND. He called a boy and told him to take my horse to the nearest stables, then he led me upstairs to the guardroom and sat me down by his brazier with a tankard of mulled wine. Once the warmth and the elixir of Aquitaine had got to work on me I found a chink of hope.

"Is the Archbishop in York?"

"Oh aye," said the guard. "He learnt his lesson last time the Scots came. This time he's stayed put in his palace."

"Have you a cloak I can borrow to cover my doublet?"

"Take your pick," he said, and threw open a coffer piled high with thick woollen cloaks for the men of the city watch.

I thanked him and set off to the cathedral close. It had begun to rain and the streets were slimy and deserted, the windows shuttered on houses that, but for Harclay, would by now have been smouldering ashes.

The Archbishop was at table when I reached the palace, so I lurked in the doorway of the great hall with some beggars who were waiting for scraps, watching the servants strut in and out carrying huge spiced fruit pies. At last an usher walked by and I was able to grab him by the sleeve.

"I must have an audience with the Archbishop," I said, and when the usher looked unconvinced and tried to pull his hand free I threw back my cloak and showed him the white hawk on my doublet.

"Ah," he said. "Wait here."

The usher walked slowly up the hall, past knights and barons whom I recognised from the refectory banquet at Byland, and round behind the high table to lean forward and whisper in his master's ear. Archbishop William glanced at me then whispered a reply, and the usher performed his languid procession in reverse. He took my arm and led me quickly down panelled passageways to the tapestried chamber where the Archbishop had received Brother Ambrose and me three years before.

"His Grace will soon be with you," he said, and left me.

I crossed to the largest window and looked out through the rain-streaked glass. The pinnacles of the Minster were invisible in the gloom. I blew on the glass and watched it mist, then the door behind me opened and the Archbishop strode in, so impatiently that he hardly gave me time to kiss his ring.

"You bring me word from Earl Andrew?" he asked.

"No," I confessed. "I came to ask your Grace for word of him. I have just reached York and heard he has been seized and proclaimed a traitor. Is it true?"

The Archbishop sighed with disappointment and sank into a chair.

"Yes, it is true."

"But he has saved the kingdom. Surely your Grace can help him?"

"He has also done something most unfortunate. He has given my Lords Pembroke and Despenser the perfect scape-goat for their defeats. They are even having it said that it was his betrayal that lost them the battle at Byland."

So it was all over. I listened to the rain beating on the windows.

"Is there no way to reach him?" I asked.

The Archbishop thumped the arm of his chair.

"Yes, that is the one thing we can still do. We can go and see him."

Within minutes I was slithering through the streets of York, out of breath as I tried to keep up with Archbishop William's purposeful strides. Behind us straggled a bewildered procession of canons and guards, wondering why they had been ordered away from their supper and quite uncomforted by the spectacle of their prelate stamping across the castle drawbridge and shouting for the grille to be raised.

Once inside the castle we got the same reply from every guard we questioned: that permission to see Harclay could only come from Hugh Despenser himself. Undeterred, Archbishop William told his escort to wait and beckoned to me to follow him, and together we climbed the wooden stairway that led up to the keep, whose slit windows squinted down at us and made me think of the chronicles of all the evil things that had happened there in the past.

Despenser received us in a large private chamber, and when he kissed the Archbishop's ring he did it quickly, without kneeling. Looking past him at his circle of attendant courtiers I saw Roland the dwarf, clutching his lute and wearing a new doublet emblazoned with Despenser's coat-of-arms. The care he took to avoid my eyes was all the proof I needed that Harclay's Fortune had ebbed away.

"What melancholy weather," remarked Despenser mockingly as our cloaks dripped puddles on the floor.

"It is no worse than the world deserves," said Archbishop William. "People are saying that you have done a wicked thing today."

Despenser affected surprise. "Then you must go into your pulpit and tell them that the wickedness is in the traitor who is being brought to justice. They should be rejoicing."

"As if they would! Harclay is a much-loved man in the North."

"I know," said Despenser mildly, "and that is why tomorrow we are taking him to London, for his trial."

"You ought to be careful, Hugh," warned the Archbishop. "You are becoming too good at leaving hatred behind you. One of these days you will have used up all England and find you have nowhere to turn."

"I thank your Grace for such considered counsel. Is that all you came to say?"

"No. I wish to see Harclay."

"By all means," said Despenser. "I'll have a guard take you down to him. I'm sure he'll be grateful for your blessing."

The dungeons were in the wettest part of the castle, where the ramparts rose sheer from the river. We were led down a dripping stairway, stumbling in the darkness each time the guard with his sputtering torch turned a corner. At the far end of an underground passage he took a resin lamp from a sconce in the wall and gave it to me to light while he unbarred a door and pulled it open for us.

Beyond the door there was a dark hole. We had to bend down to enter it, and once we were inside and tried to stand up we banged our heads on a low ceiling of dank stone and had to hunch our shoulders. Someone laughed, so close that it sounded as if the laughter was in my own head. Thrusting the lamp and its sickly glow in front of me, I all but shoved it into Harclay's face.

He was lying curled up on the floor, and even in that position he filled the chamber from corner to corner. I realised that nowhere was the cell long, wide, or tall enough for a person to stretch their full length. Harclay blinked painfully at the light and rolled over to squat on his haunches. There was a jangle of metal and I saw that his ankles were shackled.

"Robert," he said cheerily, "what a pleasant surprise. Is all well with you and Marie?"

"Oh yes, all is well . . ."

"And your Grace. I am honoured."

The Archbishop was quite overcome. "Andrew, this is

dreadful. You cannot let them do this to you. Tell them you only made the treaty to save York, and that you never intended to honour it. Crawl to them, tell them anything, but get yourself free. We need you."

Harclay scratched his head and picked things out of his hair. "I fear it's a little late for that. I made a point of telling them the truth – that I did it to show them I was not going to roll around in their filth any longer." He grinned ruefully. "Little did I realise they would shut me up in a hole like this."

"There is nothing I can do to help you," said the Archbishop. "Tomorrow they are taking you to London."

"I know," he said. "For the first time in twenty years I know what is going to happen next. It is almost a relief." He paused. "Perhaps there is something you could do for me?"

"Name it," said the Archbishop.

"Give Robert here a living as one of your scribes. He'll serve you well."

"Willingly," said Archbishop William, shifting his weight from knee to knee and uttering a most unchurchmanlike oath as he banged his elbow on the wall. "I can bear this no longer," he said, and reached forward to lay a hand on Harclay's head. "God bless you, Andrew. I will pray that your soul finds peace."

The Archbishop backed to the door and went out feet first, but not without touching me on the shoulder. "You will find me in the palace," he said. Then he was gone, and we sat listening to him groping his way up the passage.

"So go and get Marie," said Harclay, "and scribble away here in York until you have the money to go to Aquitaine. There, how does that sound for a life?"

"You found it," I said.

"Found what?"

"The one noble deed with a purpose so shining . . ." I could not say the rest. I was beginning to cry and when I opened my mouth all I could do was squeak.

"For pity's sake," he protested. "This place is wet enough already."

The guard peered in. "You've had your time," he told me.

Harclay patted my neck. "Go now, Robert. I need to sleep. The next few days could be tiring."

I nodded tearfully, flailed out with my arms and hugged him, and turned and scuffled out of the chamber. The guard slammed the door.

"Look after yourself," called Harclay, his voice no more than an echo from deep inside the earth.

The rain had stopped, and the clouds had broken to let through moonlight that was shining on the puddles of the castle yard. Rivulets of seeping water shone black on the ramparts as I plodded through the mud, wincing as my toes froze. The Archbishop and his escort had left, and in the gatehouse there was only one guard. As I walked nearer I felt him staring at me. I stared back and saw both the hooked nose that I remembered and the de Ros coat-of-arms on his jerkin. It was Girald's archer.

I stepped quickly to the right and he sprang at me, but in the instant he lunged I ducked sideways and past him. There was a splash as he fell flat in the mud, and as I hared across the drawbridge I heard him shouting Girald's name. Then I heard two pairs of running feet pounding across the drawbridge behind me.

When I reached the houses, I plunged straight into the narrowest and darkest alleyway, leaping over chicken-coops and muckheaps until I crashed into the wattle fence of a pig-pen. I flung myself sideways into a snicket between two houses and scrambled over some barrels and out into an empty street. Straight in front of me was the Carmelite monastery, but the windows were dark and the doors barred and God alone knew how long it would take the brothers to open up. Behind me I heard a splintering of wattle, a curse, and the sour grunts of an irate pig. My only hope was the cathedral close – if I could remember the way there. I ran on, turning down any street in which I could see the towers of the Minster looming ahead of me above the rooftops.

It was too long since I had eaten; my stomach churned and my legs grew clumsy. Behind me the sounds of pursuit were getting closer. I dodged round a corner into a wide street only to see a grey figure in the distance running towards me. The Minster was still several streets away. Near me was a squat-towered church, so I ran through the graveyard and grabbed the ring of the door. It was locked. I crumpled up into the drift of wet leaves on the step and lay there gasping until Girald came and dragged me to my feet.

"Where is she?" he demanded, banging my head against the door.

"This is church land," I croaked. "I claim sanctuary."

"I'll give you sanctuary," said Girald, banging my head again. "Where is she?"

The archer arrived and gave me a kick which knocked me to the ground, where I was grovelling when Girald cursed and spun on his heel. The grey figure had entered the churchyard and stopped a few paces from us, and as I peered up I recognised the gaunt face and frozen eyes of the strange Franciscan from the Forest of Galtres.

"Go away," ordered Girald. "I have no quarrel with the Order of St. Francis and no wish to start one."

"I can believe that," said the Franciscan. "You must have more than enough quarrels on your soul already. I am from one of them."

With a sudden movement he threw off his grey robes to reveal an old white surcoat emblazoned with the red cross of the Knights Templar.

"Holy Jesus," said Girald.

The archer pulled out a dagger and ran at the Templar, who drew his sword and hacked him so hard he sprawled sideways to die among the gravestones. Girald drew his sword and sprang forward, but with one stroke the Templar knocked it from his hand and with a second he plunged his own blade straight through Girald's ribs. Girald staggered backwards, crashed against the door and slid down it to land in a heap on the steps.

The Templar stood over him, waiting for him to die. Girald bled fast, and soon he had the shudders. When his teeth began to rattle he rolled his eyes and gave me a look of longing.

"Brother Scarface, give me absolution."

"I am no priest," I protested.

His mouth twisted into a gargoyle's howl of pain. I dipped my finger into a puddle and traced a cross on his forehead. "*Ego te absolvo*," I whispered, just before his limbs stopped shaking and his head lolled gently to one side.

The Templar knelt down and prayed, his sword-tip resting on the ground and the hilt pressed against his forehead. His breathing grew slower and softer and his shoulders sagged, and when at length he rose he rubbed his back like an old man and bent to clean his sword on Girald's surcoat. Only when the sword was sheathed did he notice I was still there.

"I remember your face," he said.

"You saved my life in the Forest of Galtres," I replied. "You have just saved it again."

He looked down at Girald. "That is not why I killed him. I killed him to avenge a brother."

"I know," I said. "I saw your brother die, eight years ago, the summer of the battle of the Bannockburn . . ."

"You saw him die?" asked the Templar in amazement. "It took me seven years to discover it was de Ros who killed him. His name was Simon of Antioch. He is the last of my brothers to be avenged."

I shivered at the thought of the task he had completed.

"When the persecution started," I asked, "why did you not stand together? You would have been invincible."

He shook his head. "When the persecution started we were divided and guilty. We were ripe for it."

"Guilty of heresy?"

"Yes, but of heresy not to the Church but to ourselves." Even as he spoke his stare became less frozen and his eyes softened with sorrow, as if for the first time he could look back and accept the past. "When the Holy Land fell we lost our quest, and without our quest we thought only of our power, and thinking only of our power we became the slaves of the False Wheel."

"The False Wheel?"

"The one that is known as the Wheel of Fortune."

The question to ask next was so logical and pure that I hardly dared trust it to words. "If the Wheel of Fortune is the False Wheel, what is the True Wheel?"

The Templar hesitated. "Where were you going when these men caught you?"

"The cathedral close."

"Come. I will take you there."

He picked up the Franciscan robes and led me out into the street. "What makes you talk about the True Wheel?" he asked.

"My father told me to find it, and I have been searching for it for years."

"The True Wheel is invisible," he said, "and it is different for every one of us. It is something we discover for ourselves, and I cannot tell you how to search for it."

"Then how will I know if I find it?" I wailed. "You have to tell me more."

The Templar stared at me in surprise. "All I can tell you is what it means to me, and that may mean nothing to you."

"Oh, tell me," I pleaded.

He took a long breath. "If you are a knight," he said, "you

have a choice between two roads. The first is the way of the tournament, of worldly ambition that can only be advanced by another's defeat; a life ruled by the Wheel of Fortune that gives you an illusion of mastery in the very moment that it makes you a slave. The second is the way of the quest, of the search for an ideal or the struggle to make a dream come true; a life which makes the world turn its back on you but where your steps are guided by your True Wheel, which gives you the courage to go forward even when the land is dark and the stars have lost their light."

I smiled sadly. So after all that the True Wheel was no more than some archaic concept of knighthood, a relic without meaning in the troubled realm of England.

"The quest of my Order," he went on, "was to be the keepers of the Holy Sepulchre, the guardians of the heart of Christendom. That was our dream, our True Wheel, but we lost our way. I made my vow to live for Christendom only to end my life on a quest as empty and pagan as a blood feud."

"At least it is over," I said.

"Yes," he said. "Now I am free."

We reached the gateway to the cathedral close, and there he left me. It was only later that I realised I had forgotten to ask his name.

Chapter Eighteen

LOVE'S REWARD

THREE DAYS LATER, chilled to the bone by the wind on the moors, I rode up to Rosedale Abbey. They must have seen me coming, because Marie was in the doorway to meet me, grinning impishly and covered from head to toe in the white robes of a postulant.

"Do I please you, Brother Robert?" she asked, dipping into a curtsey and laughing as I gawped at her. "Have no fear, it is only a disguise. I have not made my vows."

I was led along the cloister to meet all the nuns, and only after several minutes of gossip and giggles which would have shocked St. Bernard to his core did the Abbess offer us privacy in the chapter house.

"I have been so happy," said Marie. "The sisters are a joy. It was an inspiration that made you bring me here."

Somehow I could not pluck up the courage to kiss a girl in postulant's robes in a chapter house, so instead we sat down and held hands.

"What of you?" she asked. "Why is it that each time I see you you look five years older?"

So I told her the story of Harclay's treason, and the story of how she had become a widow. When I finished she was staring at the floor.

"Poor Girald," she said. "Even he sometimes wondered what made him so cruel. He cried when I lost the child."

"You lost his child? You never told me."

"When was there time?" She gave me a hard little smile. "So what now?"

"The Archbishop has offered me a living as a scribe, and you are free to go to Aquitaine."

She frowned. "Is that what you want?"

I looked away. "You are free. You owe me nothing."

Marie pulled my head round and stared into my eyes. "What is it? Is it the quest for the True Wheel your father told you to find? Is that what is troubling you?"

"Not any more." I told her all the Templar had said. "So you see," I ended up, "I will never find it. It belongs to the old days when there were crusades and Templars and men like my father. All I am trying to tell you is that I am not worth very much."

Her answer was to stamp her foot.

"Honestly, Robert, sometimes you cannot see the wood for the trees. Remember those stories Harclay told of the border country and how full they were of his love for the land and his sorrow at the endless devastation. He made it his quest to protect the land, and when he saw that his only hope was to end the war, he turned his back on Fortune to do it. And you, when you risked your life and came to Helmsley to find me; what was that but the quest of a true dreamer?"

All at once I thought of my father. I saw him leaving the royal court, giving up all he had for Katherine Bruce.

"Yes," I said to Marie, "you are my quest. I would do anything for you."

"Could you bear to have me with you for the rest of your life?"

I gazed at her. "I could bear the rest of my life if you were with me."

"There speaks my troubadour. Well then, your quest is only beginning."

Two days later we were back in York, dining at the house of

Eleazar David. Succulent roast mutton was followed by moist honey cakes, and when the meal was over and the children had gone to bed, Eleazar put a cherry log on the fire. Soon the room was full of its fragrance.

"So you no longer wish to go to Aquitaine?" he asked Marie.

"I am staying with Robert," she said.

He turned to me. "You will earn precious little as the Archbishop's scribe, but I can offer you work as well. I know people with private libraries, who pay well whenever they want a book copied. And you will not need to find a house; I own one over by the Baile Hill which has been empty for several years. It needs a few repairs, but I can have it ready by the spring, and you will be doing me a favour by living there."

"A favour?" asked Marie. "Oh Eleazar, you are too good."

He smiled contentedly. "It has certainly been my week for helping other people with their lives. Yesterday I had a long meeting with an old friend of Robert's called Brother Ambrose."

I thought of the Abbey of Fountains and its stricken accounts. "Did he come to sell the granges?"

"Indeed he did, but I was able to show him there was no need for that. All that needs to be done is for them to be rented out; then the tenants can worry about the harvest, the abbey will have a steady income, and the monks will be free to pursue their devotions. You could even be the one to write the deeds of tenancy."

"I would like that," I said, remembering all those days of despair in the muniment room. "I would like that very much."

The following spring, a week after Easter, Marie and I were married in the ancient church of St. Mary, a few minutes walk from our new home.

Our priest was Abbot Walter, who had travelled to York to

sign the deeds of tenancy, and our witness was Brother Ambrose, who snuffled and wiped his eyes all the way through the service. Marie wore a new gown of dark burgundy, trimmed with Venetian lace, while I, for one last time, wore the blue doublet and the white hawk of Andrew Harclay.

Then a strange thing happened. As we came out of the church the bells of the Minster began to ring wildly, sending a sound of joy up in the air to echo over the city in the spring sunshine. We saw Eleazar running towards us, laughing and waving his arms.

"Peace!" he shouted. "Pembroke and Despenser have met Bruce in Newcastle and made peace."

"Pah," said Brother Ambrose. "First they kill Harclay for doing it and now they try to steal his glory."

"I have a feeling he would laugh at that," I said. "We know the truth, that only Harclay could have shown them there was no other way."

"Perhaps you should write one more chronicle?" said Marie.

"In the meantime we have much to celebrate," said Eleazar. "If you will come to my house, the wedding feast is ready."

"A feast?" asked Brother Ambrose, his eyes glowing like a hundred candles.

We set off down towards the river. Marie held my hand, and high above our heads the bells rang the peace.

SWALLOW BOOKS

THE LAST HARPER

Julian Atterton ISBN 0 86267 184 1

This novel by Julian Atterton was shortlisted for the Young Observer Teenage Fiction Prize. Set in sixth-century Britain it tells how Gwion is forced to leave his home settlement after it is raided by sea wolves and how he finally becomes apprenticed to a master harper in the Kingdom of Rheged.

Julian Atterton is a young writer of great promise. He lives with his wife in a remote house on the North Yorkshire Moors and spends his time writing and researching into medieval history. He has studied at the Sorbonne in Paris and at the Universities of Cambridge and East Anglia. His interests include rock climbing, archaeology and acting.

THE WHITE NIGHTS OF ST. PETERSBURG

Geoffrey Trease
ISBN 0 86267 196 5

To David, arriving from America to spend a year learning Russian and assessing the business prospects for his industrialist father who had hopes of Russo-American co-operation, St. Petersburg in the autumn of 1916 was a baffling though not unfriendly city. There were disquieting undertones, odd occurrences, and always the war in the background, but David often found it hard to believe everything his student friend, Anton, told him. Before David's year was out he found himself witness to a cataclysmic event: the Russian Revolution.

Geoffrey Trease writes of the city now called Leningrad with first-hand knowledge of its exquisite river vistas and graceful buildings. He has re-created its famous 'white nights' when the sun scarcely dips below the horizon.

NO HERO FOR THE KAISER

Rudolf Frank ISBN 0 86267 200 7

The world closed in on Jan Kubitzky on September 1914 — his fourteenth birthday. Russian soldiers, armed with guns and cannon were in the fields and similarly armed German soldiers were in the wood. Between them lay the small Polish hamlet of Kopchovka, which had been Jan's home until the day when everything in it was destroyed. When the firing stopped, only he and Flox, Vladimir the shepherd's dog, were left alive.

'*NO HERO FOR THE KAISER* is a work so remarkable that you have to wonder why it has taken so long to reach us here. The German-born author served in the 1914 war, and wrote the book from that experience. It was banned and publicly burned by Hitler in 1933. Its acclaim, we learn continues . . . Graphic, memorable . . . it's clear to see why this book was put to the flames.'

Naomi Lewis *The Observer* 1986

THE SENTINELS

Peter Carter ISBN 0 86267 195 7

When John Spencer's parents die his uncle packs John off into the Royal Navy as a 'Gentleman Volunteer'. His ship, HMS Sentinel is bound for the worst service in the Navy, the West African Squadron, the anti-slavery patrol.

Torn by civil war and shattered by the impact of fire-power, the tribal organisation of West Africa is breaking down. One man taken as a slave is Lyapo, a farmer, captured by Dahomey warriors. Chained, desperate, separated from his wife and children, Lyapo is passed from trader to trader until he is bought by the ruthless American, Kimber, master of the slave-ship Phantom. Bound for the plantations of America, Lyapo now faces the hazards of the high seas where, when Sentinel and Phantom meet, he finds himself joining John Spencer in a desperate struggle for survival.

Winner of The Guardian Children's Fiction Award 1981.

SWALLOW BOOKS

THE YEAR OF THE STRANGER

Allan Campbell McLean ISBN 0 86267 199 X

The stranger came to Skye that terrible year of 1877. It was the year that Mata the tinker had died a brutal death for salmon poaching and the time, too, that a blight had fallen on the crofting village so that it seemed forever cursed. And Calum Og had been beaten senseless by his uncle, but had gained his liberty.

'Allan Campbell McLean takes as his canvas the hard, austere life led by fishermen on the Isle of Skye a century ago, and he merges with it a fascinating tale of fantasy . . . Mr McLean's skill at blending fantasy with fact is at its best.'

The Times Educational Supplement